THE RUSSIAN CHURCH

THE RUSSIAN CHURCH

By

J. N. DANZAS

TRANSLATED FROM THE FRENCH BY
COUNTESS OLGA BENNIGSEN

NEW YORK
SHEED & WARD
1936

CONTENTS

FOREWORD

When the collapse of the Tsar's empire put an end to Russian Cæsaro-papism, it seemed that the main obstacle in the way of reunion of the Russian Church with the Holy See had disappeared, but such hopes were premature, and there is no change in the attitude of the Russian Church and her faithful. Maybe this attitude is not so hopeless, and is explicable by the acute Russian nationalism which, under persecution, as well as in exile, clings desperately to a Church it identifies with its national feeling. Closer relations with Catholics may perhaps succeed in removing much prejudice, but it is necessary to establish a contact, to learn to know and understand each other, and, as things are at present, mutual understanding still seems to be very remote.

Many Russians are wont to discuss questions of religious union with a marked tendency to view it as an alliance of all Christian denominations opposed to the Roman Catholic Church. There is a group, or, more correctly, several groups, of Russian thinkers who seem to speak on behalf of their Church, though the thoughts they voice have little in common with the official teaching of the Orthodox Church as expounded by her authorized theologians. In the background, behind these intellectuals airing their private opinions, and behind the Church which is silent because she lacks a central authority powerful enough to impose her decisions upon the faithful, are the vast inarticulate masses of the Russian people who for long centuries lived in a tradition alien to these intellectuals' philosophical speculations, and yet were not over submissive to their shepherds : this is made clear by the strong sectarian movement in Russia. Thus we seem to be confronted by three different currents of Russian spirituality which at times met and mixed together, at others separated with mutual hostility and broke up into numerous streams. In order to understand these different aspects of the Russian religious mentality, it is necessary to examine its sources and analyze the different elements which went to its composition.

THE RUSSIAN CHURCH

CHAPTER I

BYZANTINO-SLAV CHRISTIANITY

VLADIMIR SOLOVIEV, in his deservedly famous book *La Russie et l'Eglise Universelle*, denounced the Byzantine origins of Russian Christianity. He, and others before him, say that her adherence to the Greek Church placed Russia, at the dawn of her national life, outside the historical structure wherein through many vicissitudes the Western Church was moulding the mentality of the peoples of Europe. This is very true, and no one will contest the paramount influence of the Byzantine spirit upon the destinies of Russia. Nevertheless, the eminent Russian philosopher's criticism of the faith the princes of Kiev received from Byzantium is unjust. It is unfair to say, as he does, that the Greek Church was withered with age, her decay poisoning the young and strong body of the Slavonic people. In the tenth century Byzantium was not in a state of decadence, and her Church, which had just triumphed over the iconoclasts, was full of life, as is amply proved by her conversion of the Slav peoples. To these semi-savages, whom she drew into the bosom of the Universal Church (for the deadly schism had not yet torn her asunder), she gave the splendours of her liturgy, the incomparable poetry of her mysticism—royal gifts to the spirit of young Russia, apt to fertilize it and make it yield the choicest fruits of a Christian civilization. The tragic and unexpected deviation of Russian history is responsible for the partial failure of these high hopes.

There is an ancient Russian legend according to which St. Vladimir, before deciding to accept Christianity, dispatched envoys into every country to study their different religions and choose the best. These ambassadors returned full of enthusiasm for the solemn worship witnessed in Constantinople : " We thought ourselves in Heaven," and these words ended the hesitations of the Great Prince of Kiev. Like every legend devoid of historical foundation, this one is typical of the frame of mind to which its invention is due, for what Russia saw in her new faith was its outward beauty, which left a permanent mark upon the Russian mind.

We must remember that this nation's conversion was not due, as in other countries of Northern Europe, to the zeal of individual apostles, great missionaries who, crucifix in hand, penetrated into dense forests to preach the gospel to wild Teutonic warriors. Russia received as her State religion the complete Christian faith with an organized and impressive hierarchy in whose wake came artists who proceeded to build magnificent churches glittering with rich mosaics. In Russia Christianity became primarily a cult appealing to the feeling for beauty, and it is thus that it entered deeply into the national soul, awakening its artistic temperament and subjugating it for good.

Yet something was lacking in this imposing worship—it had no moral depth, no power to move the soul to new duties beyond a call to sensible beauty—this is why Russian Christianity remained for so long superficial, a thin veneer of Christian ideas covering the simple and robust paganism of the masses with its superstitions, worship of the forces of nature curiously blended with devotion to the saints. It is true that three or four centuries earlier the same phenomenon could be observed elsewhere in Europe, where at first Christianity brought little change into the outlook, and especially the morality, of the newly baptized peoples. But there the Church had an unique support in the remnants of Roman civilization of which she was the heir. The floods of barbarism broke upon these fragments of the ancient municipal organization, whilst the bishop became the natural defender of his people,

B 2

not in the name of the Church only, but also on behalf of the glorious traditions of a Christianized civilization. Russia always suffered from the lack of this Roman tradition as a starting-point for her historical evolution, and during the Kiev period of her history the Russian Church never knew such a bishop—a shepherd, a defender of his flock against its foes.

The Greek clergy brought to Kiev by Saint Vladimir trained a native clergy, taught it elementary theology expressed by the Byzantine liturgy in its impressive Slavonic rendering, and this was all: for centuries no theological writings were translated except perhaps St. John Damascene's *De Fidae Orthodoxae*. The subtle dogmatic niceties which absorbed Byzantium were far beyond the untutored minds of the rough Russian warriors, whilst the clergy's moral influence was impeded by the privileged part which fell to the bishop in a State Church where his place was near the prince but far from the people, where he was a dignitary but not a shepherd.

It was the temporal ruler who spread the faith (not without occasional violence), who was concerned with a rudimentary education, who endeavoured to a certain extent to civilize the people's life. The clergy had a great part in the consolidation of the Prince's power, for it imported Byzantine notions upon the divine right of rulers and left the organization of the new Christian state to his discretion. This explains why it took Russia so long to grasp the priest's pastoral mission, and why his vocation in the eyes of her people was restricted to the celebration of the offices in all their splendour. Russian Christianity was first and foremost an imposing rite, the ministers of which were respected but not loved, and it is to this early period of national life that may be traced the origin of the two principal currents of Russian spirituality : on one hand the worship of the Church impressing its beauty upon the national soul, whilst on the other the people, in their spiritual longings, turning not to their shepherds but to the monks and anchorites.

The establishment of monasteries in Russia followed close upon her conversion to Christianity : in the time of St. Vladimir's immediate successors the great Kievo-Pecherskaya *laura* was already flourishing. Its founder, St. Anthony, and particularly his successor, St. Theodosius, have remained the outstanding figures of the infant Church ; their names, venerated through the centuries, have come down to us, whereas the names of the first bishops, even of the primates of Kiev, are known only to scholars, and discovered after much research. The holy hermits taught a contemplative mysticism, and herein lies the essential difference between Western and Russian monasticism : whereas the sons of St.

Benedict organized studies and preserved for the world the remnants of Latin culture, the Byzantine Studite "rule," adopted by the Kiev monastery, became the sole rule of all Russian religious houses. This rule taught its followers to flee the world and to despise all secular knowledge. In its aversion from the secular world Byzantine monasticism possessed a background of religious and philosophical dualism to which was due the repeated starting-up in the East of the Manichæan heresy under a variety of aspects.

The material world was uncompromisingly condemned, salvation entailed the avoidance of any contact with it, and this expression, " to save oneself" (*spasat'sia*), became the principle of religious vocation. In the monastery a man was dead to the world : St. Theodore forbade his monks all intercourse with the laity. In the caves to which the monastery owes its name (*Peshchera*—cave), pious monks revived the austerities of the fathers of the desert. This greatly impressed the people's minds, but set the holy men apart as immeasurably above the common herd. Crowds of admirers followed them and came to " save themselves " in the caves, but such men were unable to Christianize the everyday life of the people at large : the ideal was too high, almost superhuman, and there was nothing intermediate between this austere ideal and the ordinary world condemned to live " in sin."

6

Such was one of the deeper causes of the characteristic Russian tolerance towards sin of all kind. If one is not an ascetic monk there is no other choice but to be an unworthy sinner ; there is a strong temptation to sin when it is believed that *ordinary* human virtues are not conducive to salvation. The sinner can only rely upon the divine mercy, which is infinite, stretches out to the greatest criminals, and has no need of small commonplace virtues in order to save the sinner's soul ; suffice if man feels his abject unworthiness, confesses it, humbly prays for forgiveness and the intercession of our Lady and the saints —then he may live as he likes, since more or less goodness matters little in comparison with the sanctifying grace which cannot be merited in this world. This view of the relations of man to God is implicit on every page of Russia's religious history, even to our days : it has never been explicitly defined, but is nevertheless at the root of Russian spirituality, which is unintelligible unless this is understood. It is therefore imperative to examine its remote sources.

Generally speaking, the first Christian period of Russian history manifests two outstanding factors : a Church drawing her faithful by the mystical beauty of her worship but giving them no dogmatic or moral teaching beyond the liturgy in its Slavonic version, and a monastic ideal placed like an inaccessible peak far above everyday life. The time for the discussion of doctrinal questions was over, and Russians did not worry about them. The schism of 1054 had no repercussion in Russia, and her attitude towards the Latin West seemingly underwent no change, the young Russian State being closely bound to it by military and economic interests and the marriages of its princes. Yaroslav the Wise, who died in this same year 1054, married his three daughters to the kings of France, Hungary, and Norway, no religious difficulties being raised in connection with these unions, nor did the Western princesses married to Russian princes appear to have ever felt themselves in a schismatic country. St. Euphrosine, princess of Polotzk, took the veil in the twelfth century, and with the nuns of her convent went on a pilgrimage to the Holy Land, where she died in Jerusalem in 1173 and was recognized as a saint by the Latin Church.

Russian bishops were consecrated by the Metropolitan of Kiev, delegated by the Patriarch of Constantinople; but in his absence bishops of Chernigov, Volhynia and other south-western principalities went to be consecrated to the nearest Latin archbishop, as has been recently shown by a Russian historian : and such a state of things obtained until the end of the Kiev period. Had not this first and brilliant era of Russia's history ended in disaster, her religious life would probably have evolved in a Western direction, for Russia's destiny appears to have been the reconciliation between the Eastern and Western Churches. The trend of historical events destroyed these hopes. The fall of Kiev, due to internecine discord and to economic ruin when it had ceased to be the clearing-house of trade with the East (Venice and the Crusades having opened new commercial routes), and the invasion of the southern steppes by new Mongol hordes, cut off Kiev from the Black Sea. The death-blow was dealt in 1240 with the Tartars' sack of the capital, though already, in the twelfth century, Russia had begun to withdraw to the north-east, where new centres of national life formed themselves, first in Suzdal, later in Moscow : a new historical period was being inaugurated under very different auspices, the impress of which was going radically to change the people's mentality and the spirit of their national Church.

CHAPTER II

THE NATIONAL CHURCH

THE tie binding the Russian Church to Constantinople was well-nigh broken : *Tsargrad*, the imperial city, was very distant, the journey thither long and fraught with danger, sometimes even altogether impossible to undertake. With great difficulty the Metropolitan maintained casual relations with the Patriarch, and occasionally pilgrims passed through Constantinople on their way to the Holy Land. The memory of Byzantium and its splendours lived on as a kind of legend in the people's minds. They knew the golden city of their dreams had been desecrated by men from the West, and the tale of the sack of Constantinople and the establishment there of the Latin empire by the Crusaders told by distracted Greek monks to Russian pilgrims aroused intense indignation and hostility. For the first time the Latin West appeared as a world not only alien but inimical, and the further Russia withdrew into her fierce isolation the deeper this hostility grew. Gathering all her strength for a desperate struggle against the Tartar invader, she felt in her rear another menace—the Teutonic Knights and the Swedes, vanguard of the Latin world, ready to attack her.

At this crucial time, when caught between Asia and the Latin West Russia was fighting for her very existence, the Russian Church became the symbol and embodiment of the national soul. Since the Kiev period the aspect of the Russian Church had undergone a great change : she now had her own martyrs, put to death by Tartars and Finnish tribesmen, and missionaries similar to those of the Church in the Carolingian times. As the State spread northwards the meeting with pagan Finnish tribes enkindled the apostolic zeal of such monks as Stephen of Perm, Macarius Zheltovodsky, and numerous others who, cross in hand, advanced upon this new world. They brought it the gospel, the Russian language, the rudiments of a civilization ; in the forests they founded monasteries, soon to become strongholds of Russian spiritual life with all its specific features.

But this teaching, devoid of any strong theological foundation and following close upon military conquest, never penetrated deeply into the souls of these tribesmen. Baptism facilitated their superficial fusion with the Russians, whilst they retained their own heathen rites, mixing them with their conquerors' pet superstitions. At this early time Russians had already a special devotion for St. Nicholas of Myra, whom these new converts accepted as an incarnation of their new faith, invoking " Nicholas, the Russian god " together with their old idols and fetishes—and this has obtained to our days.

Nevertheless, the Christianization of these vast territories was a remarkable feat, for in less than three centuries the entire north of European Russia to the coast of the Arctic was nominally conquered for Christ, and as early as the fifteenth century the monastery of Solovki, on an island in the White Sea, became the outpost of the Russian Church. A century later the Tartar khanates of Kazan and Astrakhan were conquered, and the annexation of Western Siberia opened new and immense fields for the Church of Russia, which, protected by the imperial eagles, carried the cross to the coast of the Pacific.

But throughout those centuries and in all these vast areas Christianity was primarily a principle of Russification, the cross was inseparable from the eagles, baptism alone gave the full rights of citizenship, the Church was the symbol of nationality. To our days she retained this specific character shaped by the people's mentality in the dark times of Tartar domination, and as little in keeping with the Byzantine spirit as with the principles of catholicity at large.

To the theocratic ideal of Western Christianity Byzantium opposed a kind of religious *étatism*, though the Byzantine state was not built up on a national principle. In Russia the very idea of a state foundered in the chaos which followed the northward retreat, in the disruption of the country into virtually independent principalities, and, lastly, in the Tartar invasion. During the intermediate restless years between the collapse of Kiev and the growth of Moscow, the final fusion between the Church and the people was completed. The Church embodied the sole ideal, the only element of beauty amidst general ruin and devastation ; without her the people would have reverted to their original savagery, especially because of their inevitable intermarrying with Finns and Tartars. The complete absence of writing materials resulted in universal illiteracy, but again the Church was there to save the Russian language ; for centuries her worship was the only æsthetic expression the people knew, as her chants voiced their sufferings and hopes.

In those days the Church nurtured the great bishops who became the real shepherds of their depleted flocks. The prestige of the Prince, so great in the Kiev period, was lost in quarrels, fratricidal wars which added to the sufferings of the devastated country : sovereign princes slaughtered each other and even debased themselves to the point of seeking the Tartars' support against their brethren. Thus the people no longer saw in them their natural protectors, and clung closer to their pastors. The latter protected and comforted them, and reminded the princes of their duties, and it is especially owing to these bishops that the ideal of a national unity survived and was preached.

When the princes of Moscow became strong enough to tackle the slow and arduous task of reconstructing the Russian state, their success was assured by the Church, which supported them with all her prestige. The translation of the metropolitan see to Moscow marked the consecration of the young city and its promotion to the position of an important national centre. The great metropolitans, Peter and, especially Alexis, enforced the authority of the Moscow princes, inspired a national policy, and cemented a close alliance between the Church and the nation in the great work of political reconstruction.

The people's instinct was right ; while the memory of the " gathering " [1] princes gradually faded and their names live only in history, the great

---

[1] This term is applied in Russian history to the ruling princes of the Moscow principality—at first one of the most insignificant— who, thrifty and astute, gradually through a couple of centuries acquired, or " gathered," lands and other principalities, whereby in the fifteenth century the Great Prince of Moscow became the sole ruler of Russia. (Transl.)

metropolitans, canonized by general veneration, lived on in the people's memory, crowned with the halo of national saints, symbols of a unity reconquered and consolidated. Particularly has Alexis, adviser of the Moscow princes, organizer of the new state, father and shepherd of his flock, sharing all its tribulations, a miracle-worker revered even by Tartars, remained an ideal figure of the past, and for some six centuries his relics, kept in the monastery of the Miracle (*Chudov*) in Moscow, were a favourite shrine for Russian pilgrims, until the day when the bolsheviks desecrated them and destroyed the monastery.

Whilst the Church in the person of her bishops sanctioned the union of nation and state in one religious ideal, a profound reform was revolutionizing monastic life, that part of the Church which, as has been said, embodied in the people's eyes the moral aspect of Christianity. Monasteries had also suffered terribly—they had been plundered, their religious massacred, their books burnt. Gradually new ones took their place, for the desire to escape from the world to " save oneself " in a religious retreat was stronger than ever. But the rule had weakened, and all that survived of the old traditions was the horror of any " secular work," *i.e.*, of any activity whatever. Monasteries actually became places of retreat where often enough whole families lived together without renouncing their personal property. Monastic life was reformed by Sergius of Radonezh in the fourteenth century.

Sergius had started by living as a hermit in the dense forests which encircled Moscow ; followers gathered around him, and he decided to re-establish in all its strictness the tradition of community life based upon a spirit of renunciation and mortification. At first the monastery consisted of a few poor huts built in a clearing in the forest ; he personally felled timber for a small church dedicated to the Holy Trinity ; its vessels were of lead, its vestments of coarse linen, its liturgical books written upon strips of birch-bark. But this poverty was soon transfigured by holiness, and new disciples and pilgrims flocked to it. Sergius was not a theologian : legend asserts that only through miraculous intervention was he able to master his letters, but, like many great contemplatives, he was an admirable organizer and a profound reader of souls. It may be said that he became spiritual director of the whole of Russia, and the Great Prince of Moscow and the humblest beggar consulted him upon their spiritual needs, as well as upon questions of state. He never held any official position, having uncompromisingly refused to succeed Alexis in the primatial see of Moscow when it was offered him. His prestige gained by this refusal. Probably he never knew anything about the mendicant orders of the West, but he had the same inspired thought that the Church would be regenerated through poverty and humility. The Studite " rule "—he knew of no other—forbade a dispersion of monks for preaching, but Sergius keenly felt the influence a monk could have upon the laity by vocal teaching and spiritual direction.

Rumours of the Crusades perhaps never reached his ears, yet he admitted the necessity of a holy war upon the infidel, and when Dmitri, Great Prince of Moscow, came to ask him to bless the war which was to end in the famous victory of Kulikovo (1380), the saintly *hegumen* (abbot) replied by sending two of his monks to fight in the first ranks as a sign of heavenly assistance. This was an unheard-of action, for Russia could not understand how monks, dead to the world, could participate in battle and be killed for some temporal cause : among ecclesiastics Sergius' action was blamed, and later it even caused doubt of his qualification for canonization. But in this gesture of their beloved saint the people saw a confirmation of the complete fusion of the national and religious ideals, and the battle of Kulikovo marked its final sanction.

Even during Sergius's life the monastery of the Holy Trinity was Russia's greatest shrine. Soon it was able to make new foundations and give the impulse to the great wave of monasticism which in the following century resulted in the building of monasteries all over Russia. Sergius's spirit also inspired fervent missionaries, who founded religious houses on the desolate banks of the Volga, at the foot of the Urals, or on the coast of the Arctic ; thus was the religious life fully reinstated within the national Church. Monasteries supplied bishops, monks also in some degree took the place of the secular clergy who were uncouth, unlettered, and quite incapable of directing souls. The people became used to seeing in the monk not only an example of heroic Christian virtue, but also the counsellor and director to be consulted upon all spiritual difficulties : whereas the secular priest was merely the minister who celebrated the Liturgy, which he had memorized more or less accurately.

All contemporary documents speak of the instruction of an illiterate priest *s golosa* (*i.e.*, vocally), but, even so, it was difficult to find candidates for ordination capable of being thus coached. Often just any-one was enlisted, some poor useless creature, even a drunkard, but with a memory good enough to retain the ritual words. Even after ordination his position remained of the humblest : he led the life of a peasant and he had no access to the higher dignities of the Church, as only regulars could be consecrated bishop.

The people became accustomed to differentiate

between the Church, as represented by the higher hierarchy and the monks, and the humble parish clergy, for whom only contempt was felt, for they did not embody the idea of a Church triumphant—the crown of the State and incarnation of the national ideal.

The time came when the Church was for the first time faced with the necessity of formulating more precisely her teaching and her position in the Christian world, for in the middle of the fifteenth century she was suddenly confronted by a fact which shook her traditions and set before her problems of a general order—the question of the unity and oneness of the Church.

The Metropolitan Isidore, a Greek by birth, had taken part in the Council of Florence and signed its decrees. Russia heard, stupefied, that this council had introduced some changes in the traditional faith, and that the Greek clergy, even the Patriarch of the Imperial City, had accepted this new teaching. The people's ignorance of theology was such that they were unable to grasp what had actually happened in Florence : all they knew was that the old faith, sacrosanct and above discussion, had been modified, and the Greek clergy had a hand in this crime.

Isidore was treated as a renegade and had to flee for his life from his infuriated flock. Later, reassuring news reached Russia from Constantinople : there too the " traitors " had been exposed, the " innovations " rejected, and the old faith reinstated. . . . But a certain distrust remained in the Russian mind : Constantinople had dallied with heresy, had renounced in some way the faith of its fathers ! So it was no longer the stronghold, the glorious centre of an untarnished faith.

Shortly afterwards news of the fall of the Imperial City and its conquest by the infidel Turks reached Russia, and was considered a just retribution for a spiritual betrayal. Moscow felt itself stronger than ever, proud of its unshakable fidelity to a faith not a single jot of which could ever be questioned. No matter if the whole world turned heretic or traitor, henceforth Moscow always would be the light-giving centre of an unblemished faith, the trustee of the sacred heritage of the past, and this was the visible sign of a predestination to a greatness of which it was beginning to dream.

At the very moment when these dreams were shaping themselves with greater precision the national Church suddenly experienced an unexpected shock—heresies, hitherto unheard of, had sprung up upon the very soil of orthodox Russia.

CHAPTER III

THE THIRD ROME

In the west of the new Russian State, Novgorod, the great trading city, formed an outpost facing the Western world. It had successfully withstood the onslaught of Swedes, Teutonic Knights, Lithuania, had never known any Tartar domination, and had been virtually independent of Moscow until 1478, when Ivan III destroyed its freedom by incorporating it in the Muscovite State. Member of the Hanseatic League, Novgorod entertained active relations with Western Europe : its subjection to Russia resulted in Muscovite participation in the great city's commercial interests, but with bales of merchandize new ideas were also imported. Echoes of the religious crisis, which reached its climax at the Reformation, penetrated into Novgorod, which heard of the Hussite movement and of the spirit of criticism directed against the Church prevailing in Europe.

Suddenly and simultaneously Novgorod witnessed the birth of two sects, which spread rapidly and reached Moscow. The exact nature of their teaching has remained uncertain, because of the absence of any authentic documents. It would seem, however, that the *strigolniki* (" shorn-heads ") professed vaguely rationalist and anti-clerical tenets, whilst the others, better known and considerably more important, were called *zhidovstvuyuschie* ("judaizers"), as they taught pure unitarianism, rejecting the dogma of the Holy Trinity, the sacraments, and the veneration of saints. Horrified, the Russian Church mistook them for a reversion to Judaism, whereas they were probably only an echo of Western rationalist sectarianism which cited the Bible against the Church. The Russian Church was powerless to meet this new menace : devoid of any system of dogmatic theology, she was utterly unable to sustain any controversy, for she did not even possess a complete translation of the writings of the Greek fathers, who were known mainly by the extracts contained in anthologies. It is significant that only in the nineteenth century were the writings of the Greek fathers translated into Russian.

In the sixteenth century, in addition to the Bible, Russia possessed versions of the writings of St. John Damascene, St. John Climacus, and selections from St. Basil, St. Cyril of Alexandria, and some other fathers, chiefly from their ascetic and not their doctrinal writings, such selections being intended for monks. Besides the more popular anthologies (the *Pearl*, the *Emerald*, the *Golden Stream*, etc.) there were also numerous mediæval Byzantine hagiographies from which Russians culled ideas upon history and natural science. They still had no religious literature of their own to speak of. When, in the fifteenth century, the Solovetzky monks required a Life of their founders—Zosima and Sabbatius—they vainly appealed to Novgorod and Moscow to send them a writer able to express the reminiscences dictated by illiterate monks in a literary form : the work had finally to be entrusted to a Serbian. Given such conditions, the success of a controversy with heretics was doubtful, and it was the sudden appearance of heresies which gave an impulse to Russian theology.

The higher ecclesiastics because of this vagueness of the official teaching appear not to have manifested any strong opposition to these novel ideas : the metropolitans of Moscow were suspected of indulgence, if not of actual sympathy, towards the *judaizers ;* one of them, Zosima, even incurred the accusation of being a member of this sect.

Here we witness the first instance of the infiltration of rationalist and Protestant influences into the Russian Church, a fact upon which we shall have much more to say. The heresies were fought by the monasteries in the person of Joseph, *hegumen* of Volokolamsk, whose work *Prosvetitel* (The " Enlightener ") is a first and very feeble attempt to elaborate a theological system in Russian. Joseph appealed to tradition, supporting it by quotations from the fathers, but he failed to formulate any precise definition of the doctrine of the Incarnation, the part of the Church in the divine economy or the essence of the sacraments. Nevertheless, his zeal was genuine and, in his dread of the sectarian spirit he was unable to fight, he called upon the secular power to punish the heretics. This demand was readily complied with, and for the first time in its history Moscow saw heretical leaders burnt at the stake. Their followers dispersed into hiding, and remained there, biding their time.

Maximus, a Greek monk from Mount Athos, was invited to Moscow to translate sacred books, and he it was who supplied the Russian Church with arguments against specific heresies and heterodoxy in general. Entrusted with the revision and correction of liturgical books teeming with errors due to the ignorance of scribes, Maximus also busied himself with translations from patristic writings and with controversy. His numerous writings gave a more definite expression to Eastern doctrine. He also explained to Russians the essential difference, as he understood it, between their Church and the Catholic Church : in his opinion it was not only the *filioque* and the use of unleavened Eucharistic bread which were detestable, but the Latin spirit itself, which was, said Maximus, in absolute opposition to the true faith, for those Latins, according to him, built their system not upon the teaching of the fathers but upon the inventions of philosophers. He explained to people who had never heard the name of Aristotle that he was a pagan philosopher and a greater authority for Latins than any father of the Church. It is easy to imagine the effect of such revelations upon pious monks, whose only knowledge of paganism was the fetichism of Finnish tribes! They never doubted his word, for he had a personal experience of the mysterious and suspect West, having studied in the schools of Venice and Padua: he knew what he was talking about. This detestation of the Catholic Church, which Maximus imparted to his followers, was due, not to Byzantine prejudices only, but also to impressions received in Italy. This inveterate enemy of Rome was an ardent admirer of Savonarola, whose biography he wrote. Russia's invincible dislike and distrust of Rome, so strong as to repel every attempt at conciliation, may be traced back to the influence of Maximus.

The influence of this Greek monk upon Russian theological thought was tremendous, by far exceeding his work as translator and reviser of texts. His labours in this field came to a somewhat abrupt end: he was banished to the seclusion of a monastery because his drastic corrections of texts consecrated by long usage aroused uneasiness. Thus he fell victim of a conception he had himself done so much to foster, namely, that Moscow was henceforth sole trustee of the pure faith and of Byzantine's venerable traditions. Such was the origin of this idea; it came to fruition when Russia proclaimed herself heiress of the Byzantine empire.

In the late fifteenth century Ivan III, having married Zoe Paleologus, the last princess of the imperial dynasty, thought himself entitled to lay claims to that heritage and to the imperial eagles, which he adopted as his coat-of-arms. It was then also that Russia's arrogant motto, repeated throughout subsequent centuries, was invented: "*Two Romes fell; Moscow is the third; there can never be a fourth.*" It sounded then somewhat bumptious, but half a century later it appeared less so when Ivan IV assumed the title of *Tsar* (Czar—Cæsar), whereby he affirmed Russia's succession to the Eastern empire. On the Byzantine model, Church and State were merged into one, and the nation became identified with both.

But, however triumphant, the Church was troubled by the first attacks of heresy, and thought to meet them by educating the people and reforming the "secular" clergy. A council convened in Moscow, and known as *Stoglav* (The Hundred Chapters), energetically tackled the most urgent reforms, and also drew up a school curriculum, which at that time of widespread and crass ignorance proved unworkable. But this council's primary concern was the creation of a religious literature in the vernacular : the Church was anxious to take cognizance of herself, to intensify her teaching. Metropolitan Macarius set himself the task of composing a monumental hagiography, synthesis of all the traditions expounded by great saints, and, faithful to the Russian distinctive feature, he attached greater importance to the father's lives and examples than to their writings. Was not man's heart and not his mind the sanctuary of true faith ? *Velikyi Chetyi Mineyi* (" Great readings for the month "), Macarius's important work, was a real encyclopædia of hagiology, comprising not only the lives of saints, Eastern and Russian, for every day, but also the corresponding liturgical texts, hymns, homilies, and other fragments. This set a fashion for hagiography : every lettered person, the Tsar's son included, toyed with it, whilst *Chetyi Mineyi* remained up to the last century the beloved and familiar reading of Russians.

Oral tradition being soundly established, attention was drawn to the absence of patrology, and again Maximus the Greek came to the rescue. He had not been idle in the cell where he was confined : with helpers he had developed a considerable activity, greatly facilitated by the establishment of a printing-press in Moscow. Thus a serious campaign against the abysmal ignorance of the people was launched, the Church seemed to be quickened by a spirit of new life, strong in her close alliance with nation and state : yet certain symptoms indicated that there were cracks in the seemingly solid building.

When Joseph of Volokolamsk appealed to the secular arm against heretics, quoting the Byzantine thesis of Cæsar's absolute power, there was a strong contrary reaction within the monasteries. From the forests beyond the Volga hermits and their *hegumen* Nilus Sorsky raised their voices protesting against the interference of monks in temporal concerns, and against intolerance. By what right were heretics burnt when they ought to be prayed for, just as prayers ought to be offered for the other sinners of the world ? Secular matters were no business of monks, the religious life pursued one object only—prayer and mortification. Nilus also protested against monastic wealth, for the religious revival promoted by Sergius of Radonezh had brought to the monasteries rich donations and bequests. The admirable poverty of Sergius was forgotten : even his monastery of the Trinity (now known as *Troitzko-Serguievsky*—Holy Trinity and St. Sergius) possessed vast domains, and was not merely the greatest religious centre in Russia, but also its richest monastery.

The wealth of the religious houses was increasing, and they all owned much land.

Nilus energetically denounced this perversion of the monastic ideal : monks having died for the world, monasteries had no right to any possessions whatever. Nilus went so far as to see signs of danger in community life itself as fraught with temptations to acquire perishable things, and preached a return to the eremitical tradition of the fathers of the desert and of the first Russian monks. He and his disciples in their forest hermitages set an example of such living. With his *startzy* (elders) he practised an asceticism hostile to the world, verging on the dualism latent in Eastern Christianity. Following their lead, *startzy* in other monasteries renounced communal life entirely or partially, withdrawing into solitude and silent contemplation, the people revering them as living images of their own religious ideal. But the spirit of Sergius, who had so warmly responded to the sufferings and needs of his contemporaries, greatly weakened.

So both currents of Russian spirituality resumed their different courses. When the people's moral promptings found no satisfaction in church, they carried them to the monasteries, where they could unburden their consciences and harken to the counsels of some inspired *staretz*. But, for the time being, these two currents did not flow too far apart : the

Church was as yet too national, too close to the very soul of the people. Moreover, in the sixteenth century, her head was one of those rare men who personify a great religious ideal. Philip, *hegumen* of Solovki, whose austerities and fervour had for thirty years edified North Russia, was raised to the primatial see of Moscow. Here he took a resolute stand against Tsar Ivan the Terrible in defence of the victims of his abominable cruelty. Metropolitan Philip was indeed the faithful shepherd who lays down his life for his flock : deposed by Ivan's order and confined in a monastery in Tver, where he was strangled, he survived in the people's memory as one of their greatest saints, protector of the oppressed. They remember that he insistently claimed the Church's prerogative of intercession (*pechalovanye*) on behalf of innocent and guilty alike. This right of intercession indicated that in certain cases views held by the Church were not in accord with the exigencies of the State, a divergence as yet scarcely perceptible, yet bearing seeds of a discord which might grow and damage their intimate alliance. The people did not see so far ahead ; in their eyes Philip had been a great bishop because a perfect monk, and more than ever they were convinced that the full truth of Christ was to be found only in the monasteries at the feet of *startzy*. It was in their name that hopes for a better life were expressed.

For example, a document in circulation which to the absolutism of Moscow opposed some nebulous scheme of social and moral reform bore the names of the founders of the Balaam monastery on the lake of Ladoga (*Besieda Valaamskikh Chudotvortzev*)— " Discourses of the miracle-workers of Balaam ").

But this monastic ideal was far beyond the average man : even in religious houses not every aged monk was a *staretz*. The latter commanded such veneration precisely because they presented isolated cases of holiness. Another type of sanctity deeply impressed the popular mind : the *Yurodivye*—" fools for Christ's sake," mostly one-time " novices " unable to stand the confined life of the monasteries. They remained in the world in absolute poverty, practising extremes of humility and every privation, but exercising a right to speak out the truth fearlessly and in any circumstances. Untrammelled by any conventions, living upon alms, clad in rags, despising both worldly goods and personal cleanliness, these people journeyed from shrine to shrine, or wandered about the cities as their fancy prompted them, surrounded by a superstitious awe. The best known of these men was Vasily (Basil) the Blessed, whose name has reached us because of the grand church of our Lady near the Kremlin, built in his honour by Ivan the Terrible. Another *yurodivy*, Nicholas, dubbed the same Tsar a " cannibal," an insult the sovereign swallowed in silence because he, too, shared the popular superstition in regard to these "holy fools." This peculiar form of holiness was also an echo of Byzantium, but whereas there it appeared only in rare and separate cases, in Russia it suited the people's nomadic tastes and was of very common occurrence, even among women.

But even under this shape the ascetic ideal was inaccessible to ordinary people, for whom a Christian life meant attendance in church and pilgrimages to remote monasteries and other centres of religious life. People went there to breathe a whiff of holiness, but no sooner had the pilgrim left the threshold of the sanctuary than he reverted to the coarse wickedness of his everyday life, to the drunkenness and debauchery which so shocked foreign travellers in Russia. Tolerance for every sin prevailed : why try to improve a little since one could never hope to be really righteous ? Better to hope for divine mercy and the intercession of innumerable saints devoutly invoked. The Church, which was beginning to concern herself with dogmatic questions, took no heed of moral theology ; as long as a man was a good enough Christian to come to church it mattered little if he were also seen sprawling dead drunk in the gutter or killing somebody in a brawl : he was a poor sinner, sure of divine forgiveness if truly humble of heart.

This curious conception of humility, divorced from any moral background, was becoming a characteristic feature of the Russian mentality, and will be encountered later under a variety of aspects. Never did the Russian Church teach any distinction such as that between mortal and venial sin : she was sure of the salvation of all her children, upon whom she bestowed the priceless heritage of a pure faith untainted by heresy.

In 1589 the idea of Moscow as centre of this one true faith received its final consecration when her metropolitan was raised to the rank of patriarch with the sanction of the four Eastern patriarchs, who now looked to Moscow and her mighty Tsar to protect Eastern Christendom. Moscow, with its patriarchal see, became the equal of Byzantium, and the prophecy of the Third Rome was fulfilled. It was at this time that the conquest of Siberia opened vast new prospects for State and Church alike, and no one suspected the proximity of a disaster which was to deal a deadly blow to the Church.

The century which separated the establishment of a patriarchate in Moscow and the terrible crisis of the *raskol* (schism) is considered by Russians to have been the golden age of their Church : they idealize it, saying it embodied a principle altogether national, religious, and political. Russian thought has borne so strong an impress of this ideal to our own days that it is necessary to sketch the history of its formation and crystallization. For Western Europe the sixteenth century marks a time when nationalism asserted itself outside the frame of mediæval Christianity, and finally disrupted it by subjecting the religious principle to the interests of a national State. For Russia it was, on the contrary, a time of triumph for a religious ideal identified with the national principle, a fact which influenced Russian thought then beginning to evolve independently of the Church.

CHAPTER IV

THE GREAT SCHISM

WE have seen Russian national instinct identify itself with the Church, and the religious idea become a political ideal. But in order to assert itself fully a political conception has to be opposed by some contradictory notion, by a different solution to the given problem. The only opposition the Christian Church, universal by her very essence, knows is that between the temporal and eternal. Necessarily Russian religion, when it became a political ideal, had to seek for an opponent in order to affirm itself, and it found this opponent in the Catholic Church.

Until this time the Orthodox Church of Russia had fought against the " Latin spirit " in general, entrenching herself behind her traditionalism in order to safeguard herself from its influence. But at the time when Moscow began to realize the part it was to play, and its ambitions awoke, the Latin world as a whole was no more. In the great theological disputes of the Reformation all the traditions and dogmatic teaching of the Russian Church should have shown her that innovations were undermining the very foundations of Christianity, yet never did Moscow repel Protestant infiltration as uncompromisingly as she repelled every step Rome made towards a better understanding. Naturally Russian theological ignorance weakened the influence Protestant propaganda might have had, but there was a hazy intuition that Protestantism supported the thesis of a Christianity wherein the national principle took precedence over the universal. In the throes of her religious crisis Europe failed to perceive at first the strength of nationalist currents behind the struggle against Rome, but in Russia the narrow circle of theological speculation allowed play to that intuition and to sympathies with the wreckers of the Latin world who were fighting Catholicity in the name of nationalism. Bound up with a political ideal, Russian Christianity was losing the notion of the true nature of the Church.

From the political viewpoint Protestant sects presented no danger to Russia, whereas she saw in the Catholic Church the ally of Poland, her old enemy. In the seventeenth century the Russo-Polish conflict had reached its climax, fixing that hatred [1] of the Catholic Church which is typical of the Russian mentality.

---

[1] We use this word *hatred* not in the sense of its being a tenet of the Russian Church but a popular attitude due to ignorance. The form of Russian religion is more emotional than reasoned, and so this word expresses best a feeling of violent repulsion. This historical analysis of the Russian mentality shows how circumstances have influenced its attitude up to the present day.

Ever since the late sixteenth century this hatred had been kept alive by a movement both political and religious, which led to the creation of a Uniate Church in Poland which took from the Russian Church considerable numbers of her children. We must remind our readers that, following upon the downfall of Kiev, much of its former territories had been gradually absorbed by Lithuania, the people retaining their Slav-Byzantine Church under rulers who were pagan until 1386, when a marriage with Queen Hedwig of Poland brought Prince Yagello of Lithuania into the Catholic fold. Notwithstanding years of uninterrupted alliance with Poland and strong Latin influence, religion in Lithuania remained more influenced by Russia than by her Western neighbours. In the sixteenth century Protestant doctrines penetrated into both Poland and Lithuania, and met with great success among the upper classes ready to follow the example of their Prussian neighbours : the saving of both countries for the Faith is almost entirely due to the Jesuits. When the fusion of Lithuania and Poland into one State was sanctioned by the Act of Union of Lublin in 1569, the religious question became an acute problem of internal policy, since a great part of the subjects of this new Catholic State were bound to Russia by ties of blood and a common Church. The difficulties increased when Moscow, faithful to its label of the "Third Rome," established its own patriarchal see and proclaimed itself the religious and political heir of Byzantium. For those beyond the Russian border the problem could be solved only by a *rapprochement* with the Holy See. A union, closely following the lines of the Council of Florence, was promulgated in 1596 at Brest-Litovsk, whereby the Catholic Byzantine Church of Poland came into being. This Uniate Church has survived to our days, though it suffered much both at the hands of Polish magnates, who despised it as a *khlopskaya vyera* (religion for serfs), and at the hands of Russians for whom Uniates were renegades more detestable even than Latin Catholics.

This hatred only increased in the early years of the seventeenth century when Russia and Poland were locked in a death struggle. When, after the extinction of the old dynasty, "pseudo-Dmitri" ascended the throne of Moscow he paid for Polish support by marrying a Polish Catholic and by his own "apostasy" : this betrayal of the national ideal cost him his life. Immediately afterwards Russia was plunged into the anarchy of the *Troubled Times*, when Moscow was held by a Polish army and the country torn by civil war—it was then that the Church saved the country by proclaiming and directing a "holy war." This the people never forgot, and it was to the Church, more than to military leaders, that the honour of victory and the mass-rising against the invader were due. Patriarch Hermogene's flaming appeals and his subsequent murder by the Poles, the heroic resistance of the monastery of St. Sergius, which put heart into the Russian forces at the crucial moment, these lived in the nation's memory.

When the storm which had nearly wrecked Russia subsided, Church and nation were united in the people's worship, and the accession of the Romanovs seemed only to consolidate this alliance of Church and State, the Government being in the hands of the patriarch, father of the young Tsar Michael.[1]

A clear result of these years of trouble was a recrudescence of hostility towards the Catholic Church, henceforth considered Russia's bitterest enemy, a hostility felt also by the people living on the lands which under the peace treaty with Poland were ceded to that State : even such purely Russian towns as Smolensk were incorporated into Poland. And among these new Polish subjects, men who had defended Smolensk and who had harkened to the call of the monks of St. Sergius, now belonged to the

[1] Theodore Romanov, an extremely able and astute nobleman, was compelled to enter religion under the name of Philaret by Tsar Boris Godunov, who feared the Romanovs, allied to the old dynasty, as potential rivals. He would have been the actual candidate for the throne but for the fact that a monk was ineligible, so his son Michael, aged 16, was elected Tsar, Philaret being raised to the patriarchal see. If the weak and dull-minded Michael was *de jure* tsar, his brilliantly gifted father was the sovereign *de facto*. (Transl.)

diocese of Polotzk, whose bishop, St. Josaphat, was an indefatigable apostle of the union. . . . The results are well known : in 1623 the glorious bishop was killed, and the Polish Government's terrible reprisals against his murderers only widened the chasm separating Russia from the Catholic Church.

Nothing happened to assuage this hatred ; relations with Poland assuming the character of chronic warfare, and, as the strength of Russia grew, lost territories were gradually regained, Kiev reconquered through an alliance with the Cossacks of the Dniepr, the " Uniate " problem only became more acute. Every step taken by Russia in her slow westward progress corresponded to an increasingly bitter conflict with Catholicism, and bloody persecution of " apostate brethren." But at the very time when Kiev, *mother of Russian cities*, was recaptured, the Russian Church experienced the beginning of a great crisis which undermined her vitality and eventually broke the ties binding her to the nation.

Patriarch Philaret Romanov had been co-ruler with his son Tsar Michael, appending his signature after the Tsar's to all official acts, and so until his death in 1633 he was a living symbol of the sacred union of Church, State, and nation. None of his successors could inherit his prestige, and Patriarch Nikon, anxious to regain it, only precipitated the explosion of disruptive forces, the very existence of which had been unsuspected ; he was opposed both by a Government jealous of its authority and by a people angry with their shepherd.

The drama of Patriarch Nikon is the turning-point in the slow evolution of the Russian Church which had blended into one the religious principle and the national instinct. As has been said, in the sixteenth century the solid structure of Church, State, and nation showed some cracks which had seemingly disappeared owing to subsequent events : but in the second half of the seventeenth century the change in the appearance of this structure was obvious. It was due to several causes. The wall which separated Russia from the outward world had collapsed, she was entering into a new period of her history ; she was no more an isolated world but a factor in Europe's political life. Foreigners flocked to Moscow as military instructors ; they were to be found at court ; English and German traders competed in activity ; Dutch and particularly German merchants in Moscow even occupied an entire suburb, the famous *Niemetzkaya Sloboda*, where, shortly after, Peter the Great would pass his turbulent youth in unedifying carousals.

The Russian upper classes were yielding to the spell of the new world which now was revealed to them, and ideas of which the truth had never been questioned were being discarded. The masses were hostile to, and distrustful of, anything coming from abroad, but doubts about principles hitherto taken for granted let loose in their midst obscure forces of anarchist individualism. Thus the Church was faced by unexpected changes in the life of Russia over which she was losing control. It was Nikon who accelerated the final disruption.

In order to realize the inevitability of the tragedy it suffices to note how its principal actors neither wished nor foresaw it. Tsar Alexis [1] was the most devout sovereign Russia had ever known, and certainly one of her most truly national rulers ; by a cruel irony of fate he was to play a fatal part in the destinies of the Church he was devoted to and destroy the unity of the national principle which he was sincerely anxious to safeguard. Patriarch Nikon, considerably above the level of the average Russian bishops, was a man of great learning, austere life, and profoundly devoted to his Church : this very superiority was the cause of his tragedy. Among those who, on behalf of the national religion, protested against innovations were many generous men moved by sincere piety and genuine love for the religious ideal of their country. But history was in contradiction with this ideal, and was to belie it cruelly ; the collapse of the imposing edifice of nation, State, and Church was so sudden as to prove

[1] Michael's son (1629–1676).

that hidden disruptive forces had been at work for a long time.

The thunderbolt fell when a revision of the liturgical books was undertaken, a century after the failure of Maximus the Greek's efforts. As in his days, this provoked a storm of accusations of sacrilegious tampering with sacred texts, and the personal unpopularity of the man who was behind these innovations added to the bitterness of the denunciations. The people respected their bishops in so far as their utterances reflected monastic ideals, but such was not the case with Nikon. Like the beloved Philip, he, too, had been *hegumen* of Solovki, where he gained no halo of holiness but only the hostility of his monks because of too arbitrary attempts at reforms. Later he even founded a rival monastery near Solovki (Holy Cross, on another island of the White Sea) with the avowed intention of competing with the older foundation. Now Solovki was one of the most popular shrines, and pilgrims brought back to Russia tales of the monks' rancour against their late abbot, now Patriarch of All Russia. In Moscow, where Nikon enjoyed the favour of Tsar Alexis, he had many enemies owing to his domineering and arrogant ways. His zeal for the regeneration of the Church, and his fight against ignorance, had antagonized many ; when he appealed to the great traditions of Greek theological science his foes scented heresy. It had become so natural to consider Moscow the centre of true faith that Greeks were looked upon with contempt—had they not betrayed Orthodoxy at Florence? The Church was not Greek but Russian, and would have nothing to do with any alien inspiration : she had her own national traditions, and yet Nikon, a Russian of the Russians, dared declare himself Greek by his intellectual affinities !

Such grievances alone were insufficient to bring about the catastrophe : the part played in the conflict by a traditionalism outraged by the revision of forms of worship has been grossly exaggerated. It is overlooked that widespread ignorance could scarcely result in so great a respect for the written word, especially since a considerable part of the clergy received only aural instruction. The celebrated *chelobitnaya* (petition) which Solovki addressed to the Tsar, protesting against the patriarch's innovations, was signed by a few score monks on behalf of a large community, the greater part of whom were unable to write their own names, and these illiterate men are supposed to have been qualified to criticize sacred texts ! Admitting, and this is undeniable, that among the religious there were fanatics blinded by their very ignorance, still the great motive-power behind *raskol* (schism) was not excessive conservatism. When the flame of dispute was fanned into a great conflagration, when millions repudiated the authority of the State Church, it soon became apparent that the dissidents were in no wise inspired by a conservative spirit. The *raskol* was unable to preserve the unity of faith; it immediately crumbled into fragments, each reflecting some particular religious angle. An uncompromising traditionalism turned the slightest word or gesture into a matter of rigid doctrine, such as the number of fingers to be joined in the sign of the cross, the number of alleluias to be sung, the wearing of a beard, and so forth. Another rationalist current was reminiscent of Protestant teachings, the infiltration of which into Moscow had never stopped ; there were also mystics claiming the supremacy of individual alleged inspiration independent of any doctrinal authority. Though it was only much later that many of these sects assumed an explicit form, in this first rebellion against the established Church their different tenets were all implicit.

This religious crisis coincided with a revolutionary movement the periodical outbursts of which shook the State like an earthquake. The re-adaptation to novel political conditions, the re-organization of the State in conformity with new demands awoke slumbering nomadic instincts, strongly tinged with anarchy : they manifested themselves in the Moscow disturbances and the rebellion and massacres

45

organized by Stenka Razin. In earlier times the old Muscovite State kept these subversive instincts in check, though it never eradicated them, because, despite a despotism occasionally brutal but really superficial, it actually allowed much individual freedom. Moreover, in those days the stronghold of the State stood encircled by vast uninhabited lands where rebellious elements found a safe refuge. Now these desert regions were being gradually absorbed, and lawless people, such as the Cossacks, subjected to control. The requirements of taxation, recruitment of a regular army, organization of trade and export, diplomatic relations—all these new exigencies demanded a radical reconstruction of the State in order to bring it into line with the States of Western Europe. For Russia, which never experienced the evolution of the feudal system and had not been grounded upon the foundations of Roman law, this adaptation to Western European standards was and has ever been her great tragedy, a fact which soon became apparent. When the ship of the State directed its course westwards the people immediately felt instinctively an ideological break with the past, and their reaction to this betrayal took the shape of a violent opposition against anything bearing the stamp of novelty and of anarchical excesses. In either case they were unconsciously moved to safeguard their psychological independence against an

46

alien spirit. The Church was in a dilemma : in its inevitable westward drift the State had left her lagging behind, with all her traditional horror of the Latin world, yet in order to fight the State she would have to affirm rights deriving from the Christian conception of the Church, and every definition of such rights was of necessity but an echo of the Catholic doctrine she had so often denounced. Moreover, faced by rebellious children with demands for freedom of personal judgment, she was unable to claim authority and enforce discipline without denying the ideal of a national and popular religion she herself had done so much to foster. And this Church, Rome's irreconcilable foe, was now being accused of " Latinism," when actually endeavouring to rediscover the true basis of her own doctrine. The hatred of the Catholic spirit that she had fomented was now being directed against herself : *raskol* was a judgment pronounced against the Church of Russia as a whole, against her national exclusiveness, against the particular mentality she had imparted to the people to the exclusion of Christian Catholicity.

At first Nikon obtained the condemnation of his chief adversaries, but the anathema pronounced against *raskol* only served to deepen the gulf separating the State Church from the national religion, which entrenched itself as in a hostile camp. Then followed the struggle between the hierarchy and the

State, a struggle in which the Church which had identified herself with the State had no doctrinal support. The tragedy proceeded swiftly, ending in the condemnation of Nikon, disowned by his Church which was bowed under the secular arm. The servile attitude of the other Eastern patriarchs in this emergency showed Nikon the impossibility of carrying on the fight. There is an old tradition according to which the patriarch had thought of appealing to the Pope's jurisdiction, but this is doubtful, for the hopelessness of any Roman intervention was only too obvious. But Nikon's suggested establishment of a separate ecclesiastical province under his own jurisdiction, independent of the patriarch who was to replace him at Moscow, was considered to bear the mark of Roman influence.

A century earlier Philip had fallen victim to an arbitrary act of tyranny : Nikon succumbed in an ideological conflict and his drama was that of the Russian Church as a whole. Deposed, and banished to a remote monastery, the patriarch who had laboured for the regeneration of his Church witnessed the victory of that Cæsaro-papism which consummated the absorption of the Church by the State.

Raskol thought it had broken away from the Nikonian Church, whereas actually it had to deal with a Tsarist Church. When religious opposition assumed the character of a rebellion, the State hit out and the people, wont to seek in the monasteries for the true spirit of their religion, witnessed an unbelievable thing—those monasteries in open war against Moscow, and Solovki, the great northern shrine, besieged by the forces of the Most Orthodox Tsar. It sustained an epic siege for ten years, was captured, plundered, and its monks put to the sword, and a cry of horror rang throughout the land of Russia. Fires were set alight, not as of yore for the burning of heretics, but for the execution of such men as the Archpriest Avvakum, who seemed to embody the very spirit of the old national religion. . . .

Half of the population was now outside the Church, the people who followed their own religious traditions hating the official organization which, as handmaid of the State, would inevitably follow the westward trend.

In this flotsam the State picked up all fragments of the past that suited its new orientation : the old national arrogance, the dream of the *Third Rome*, stripped of its religious meaning and transformed into an imperialist ideal, the traditional hatred of Catholic Rome. For the last there was a new reason : the name of Rome recalled strife between the Church and the Empire, and Roman influence would sooner or later revive an acute problem, the danger of which had been quite recent. Thus the evolution which secularized the Russian State, directing it westwards towards the dreaded Latin world, had to seek allies in the western elements inimical to Rome : such was the religious policy of Peter the Great, under whose reign the tragedy of the Russian Church was completed.

CHAPTER V

THE SYNODAL CHURCH AND LAY SOCIETY

At the very moment when the final disintegration of the block of State, nation, and Church left the last disarmed and with the ground cut from under her, an opportunity arose whereby she could consolidate her theological teaching.

Kiev, now again a Russian town, was an important centre of studies : Peter Moghila, its celebrated metropolitan, gave a strong impulse to the study of theology, and the academy which bore his name and was modelled on Jesuit colleges became the nursery of churchmen. It had a branch in Moscow at the end of the seventeenth century in a school which subsequently became the great Ecclesiastical Academy. But the Russian Church considered the writings of Peter Moghila too markedly tainted with " Latinism," his interpretation of Eastern theology too openly stressed the identity of the doctrine of the Eastern Church with teachings repudiated as " Roman doctrine." The school of Kiev, being suspect, had no decisive influence upon Russian theology, and the Russian Church dared not fathom her own doctrine lest she should recognize in it things pertaining to Catholic beliefs. The State monopolized the teaching of theology in the schools, over which the Church retained only a purely nominal control.

Such was for nearly two centuries the situation of the Church in Russia. In the years immediately following upon the schism it had not yet crystallized, but it was obvious that the Church was powerless to fight tendencies which were gradually depriving her of all her rights against the State, and was rapidly becoming secularized. The two last patriarchs restricted themselves to timid protests, of which no heed was taken, and when, upon the death of Patriarch Adrian in 1700, Tsar Peter cancelled the election of his successor, the non-existence of any head of the Church passed nearly unnoticed. The will of the monarch stood in the stead of all ecclesiastical traditions, and the Church, like the people, became a passive object for the formidable reformer's experiments.

Twenty years passed before the position of the Church was finally settled, for only in 1721 was the institution of the *Most Holy Synod* decreed. It was intended to replace the abolished patriarchate. During these two decades Peter's thoughts seemed to have wavered between different solutions of this problem of the organization of the State Church : on several occasions it was thought in Europe that time was ripe to draw the Tsar's attention towards union with Rome, and Peter willingly conversed on the subject with the Jesuits he encountered on his journeys or with doctors of the Sorbonne. These hopes show how ignorant the West was of the actual position in Russia. Any closer *rapprochement* with Rome would have provoked an explosion of hatred among the people and in the Church, and the Tsar, however ruthlessly he might fight the bitter hostility of the people against his reforms, would certainly never have dreamt of further embittering the struggle by an introduction of religious controversy. Common detestation of Catholicism might have brought together the official Church and *raskol*, a reconciliation which would not suit Peter, his policy being to treat *raskolniks* as rebels, thus facilitating the enslavement of a Church deprived of any popular support. Moreover, the Tsar was well aware of the fact that the Catholic spirit would not fail to renew the struggle between Church and State, the fear of which haunted him. If in abolishing the patriarchate he had destroyed the organization of the Church, it was certainly not with the object of encouraging the adherence of Russia to the great system headed by Rome. Peter realized the power of Rome, and to conciliate her and enlist her support in matters of foreign policy he considered it expedient to hint occasionally at the possibility of a religious understanding, but it was a thing he actually never desired at all. His real object was the complete secularization of the State, and if for twenty years his plans as to the future of the Church were unsettled, this was because he envisaged the possibility of doing without any Church at all.

What Peter did encourage in Russia was scepticism and irreligion, characteristic traits of the Russian intellectual class during two centuries. It is true that occasionally he did revert to the outward practices of religion, but this was either because of some passing superstitious mood or was dictated by political considerations. His true views of religion expressed themselves in the blasphemous buffooneries which he so carefully organized. Let us make no mistake : these abominable revelries were not merely an outcome of coarseness nor the accessories of the drunken orgies beloved by Peter and his "eaglets" : deliberately, and with cool calculation of their effect on the people, Peter arranged all the details of the ignoble processions which mocked at Christianity, the Church, and the sacraments. The place of honour was given to the "most drunken and most ribald college of cardinals," presided over by a "prince-pope" seated upon a hog. . . . These horrors culminating in a blasphemous "Mass to Bacchus."

These insults to the Catholic Church were carefully thought out, Peter's brutality masking the foresight of his genius. He had an intuition of the inherent unity of the Church despite apparent enmities and discords; therefore, he realized that war had to be waged against the Universal Church, his ultimate goal being a completely secularized and anti-Christian society. But his henchmen, initiated to irreligion, comforted themselves with the delusion that the insults were being heaped not on their national faith but on the Catholic Church, and the participants of the hideous orgies felt no scruples in fulfilling their customary religious duties and even going to the sacraments. In this they only followed their master's lead. The clergy was dumb, priests carried out their priestly duties, gave communion to anyone who wished to receive it. . . . Let us remember the traditional tolerance of sin typical of the Russian Church. Gently she was slipping into indifference, whilst Russian society was entering into a period when a profound divergence existed in minds contaminated by atheism and the habit of certain customary religious practices considered chiefly as national symbols.

The people believed Peter to be anti-Christ, and detested his person and his entire work. The Tsar who trampled upon every sacred tradition, who desecrated the Church, melted bells to make guns, insulted monks, enlisted novices in his army, compelled men to shave off their beards, heavily taxed recusants—that Tsar in his foreign garb could only be a scion of Hell. Innumerable martyrs witnessed to this belief with their blood.

In shedding blood Peter was not squeamish, and the long struggle he sustained against his own people assumed the character of a veritable persecution. Years passed by without assuaging the savagery of the struggle, till at last the fierce reformer realized that nothing could uproot religion from the national soul. The people's revolt found an echo in the Tsar's immediate surroundings, and he was able to appreciate the scope of the opposition when he saw his own son as an enemy, plotting against him on behalf of the old national ideals. The trial of Tsarevitch Alexis (1718) called a halt in Peter's religious policy. Since this national religion was seemingly ineradicable, it had at least to be enslaved, made completely subservient to the needs of the State : thus the plan of a synodal organization was elaborated, and three years later brought into being. It bears such glaring evidence of Protestant influence that it was considered to prove Peter's personal Lutheran sympathies. But this is wrong : Peter was quite as indifferent to Lutheranism as he was to Catholicism. He had a sweeping contempt for any dogma whatever, and was refractory to Christian morality in general : all he wanted was a secular State. A national Church being inevitable, a Protestant organization was a lesser evil, and Peter was too far-sighted not to perceive it to mean the victory of the State. In Theophanes Procopovitch he found the man to further his plans—an apostate Catholic who reverted to Orthodoxy by way of Lutheranism, a worshipper of the powers that be, ready to perpetrate any perfidy ; it was this man, raised by Peter to the archbishopric of Novgorod, who became the Tsar's zealous collaborator in the drafting of the famous *Ecclesiastical Regulations*.

Though for a long time Protestant ideas had been insinuating themselves into the Russian Church, yet hitherto their assimilation had been unconscious. When they became more explicit and a grave menace to the doctrinal integrity of the Church, a reaction against them was attempted : it was headed by Stephen Yavorsky, metropolitan of Riazan and *locum tenens* of the patriarchal see, the only scholar and theologian the Russian Church possessed at the time. He wrote a refutation of Procopovitch's Protestant views, but in vain, as the Tsar, perfectly aware of what he was about, protected Theophanes, so that Yavorsky's important treatise *Kamen Vyery* (Rock of Faith) never saw the light during his lifetime, and was published only after Peter's death. It came too late, and had no influence upon the Church now firmly established upon Protestant foundations : but for us it is a valuable witness to the doctrine of the Russian Church as faithful to the traditions of the Eastern Orthodox Church and free of any alien accretions.

The institution of the synod rang down the curtain upon the crisis which had torn the Church ever since the days of the great schism, and she was now reduced to being a cog in the complex administrative machine elaborated by Peter. The lower clergy became simply employees entrusted with police functions, bound to violate the secret of the confessional every time that the safety and interests of the State were involved ; above them the bishops were converted into important officials primarily concerned with the interests of the State ; lastly, the government of the Church was assigned to a synod, or, more correctly, a committee of bishops, appointed by the Tsar and presided over on his behalf by a lay official.[1] Throughout the next two centuries the Russian Church will have no history proper, for her history is that of the State.

---

[1] The chief procurator of the Holy Synod was never its actua president, a function which nominally belonged to the sovereign and symbolized by the empty chair at the meetings. The sovereign being permanently absent, the first place belonged to the metropolitan of St. Petersburg. Thus, legally speaking, there was no president, though actually the chief procurator, " the sovereign's eye," conducted the debates. All such formalities were dropped outside the official sittings when the chief procurator became the virtual dictator in every sphere of ecclesiastical life. Whilst the metropolitan saw the emperor only on ceremonial occasions, the chief procurator was privileged to make a personal report like all other ministers of the crown.

At a first glance it seems surprising that this tremendous change should have made no great impression upon its contemporaries ; the *raskolniki* (schismatics), who from the days of Nikon were wont to see nothing but abomination in the official Church, perceived no sensible difference between radical changes affecting the very structure of the Church and their old grievances against the three fingers' sign of the cross and threefold alleluia. The upper classes laboured under the illusion that their new Church was identical with that of metropolitan Philip and Sergius of Radonezh—the impressive liturgy remained unaltered—and for them the liturgy was religion itself. More than a century had to elapse before the question of religion became a painful problem of Russian philosophical thought.

But neither in Peter's days nor in those of his immediate successors did questions of philosophy awaken any interest, the intellectual élite, educated by the great reformer, was still at its " primer " stage of development. But besides this ignorance there was another and deeper cause which explains the facility with which the most enlightened Russians accepted the new position of the Church : this was the decline of religious feeling undermined by the revolution which Peter effected in the realm of thought and of morals, especially by Western influence, which now dominated Russian intellectual life. For centuries the Latin West had been unknown to Russians, and now when they took a leap into the Western world they encountered the Europe of the eighteenth century, de-Christianized and rabidly anti-Catholic.

Their closest contact was with Holland and Protestant Germany, where they could only learn enmity towards the Roman Church. The sailor or diplomat who journeyed to England found that there too anti-Catholicism was rife and a national characteristic. Even France was Gallican, Jansenist, and free-thinking, the France of the *Lettres Persanes*, the country where Voltaire had already seen the light. Formerly Catholicism was abhorred as the ally of Poland, now it was seen humbled, criticized, persecuted or disdainfully cast aside as antiquated and quite unworthy of an enlightened age. The Russians, like all newcomers to civilization, were anxious to appear up to date, and hastened to enlist under the banner of free thought. If at home they still kept up some outward religious appearances, abroad they flaunted their irreligion, except when Orthodox worship flattered the national pride which they still preserved, despite an often childish admiration for European culture. In this culture they failed to see the Catholic Church's age-long influence, and Europe's past history was for them a closed book. French agnosticism of the eighteenth century allied itself with Protestantism to denounce the Catholic Church as the enemy of knowledge and thought, a sinister obscurantist power which had for centuries oppressed mankind, and whose yoke had at long last been shaken off. This state of mind has to be understood in order to comprehend the influence it exercised over generations of Russian " intellectuals," who finally lost every notion as to the place the Church held in society. Because of this they were unable to detect in the organization of the Russian Church those features which perverted the very essence of ecclesiastical principles. Above all, this mentality, grafting itself upon the perennial hatred of " Latinism," has made any understanding of Catholic ideology and doctrine impossible down to our own days. The insurmountable wall between the Russian religious consciousness and the Catholic idea is purely a matter of misconception.

Until the eighteenth century the Russian attitude was governed by political hostility and naïve ignorance. As Russia developed into a great Power, with no formidable Catholic adversaries, the former decreased, but ignorance increased and became conscious. Russians would not know the Catholic Church, took no trouble either to study or even to fight her—she was seen only through the scoffing of libertines and Protestant pamphleteers. Thus was moulded a mentality which to this day is responsible for the perversion of the idea of the Catholic Church which prevents Russians from perceiving her inward mystical life, the sanctifying grace which illumined so many souls even in the worst days of widespread agnosticism. At the same time, this ignorance of the Universal Church and her eternal truths finally obliterated in Russia all true notion of the Church in general. The intellectual classes lost all consciousness of the doctrinal unity of the Church. Seen from outside, the Russian Church was now but another Government department : for her children she was a venerable tradition inseparable from an arrogant nationalism.

In order to gauge this deep ignorance of Christian principles, it suffices to note that even in Protestantism, now far nearer to the trend of Russian thought, the latter saw only its outward aspect, its national principle and anti-Catholicism, overlooking the moral theology Protestant denominations could have taught it. Peter the Great, refusing to Lutheranize Russia completely and officially, showed the perspicacity of his anti-Christian rationalism. Even under the shape suggested to him by Leibnitz—the union of all Churches in a mitigated Christianity emptied of dogmatic formulæ—there was a basis of moral teaching that Peter was in nowise anxious to encourage in his Church. Isolated from the great traditions of Christianity, many of which survived in

Protestantism, the Russian Church would slide more easily down the slope of her traditional tolerance of sin, and this suited admirably the libertinage of the new Russian society.

Peter achieved his aim : under the shadow of a national Church completely enslaved by the State an entirely secular mentality was moulded, and it was to guide the religious destiny of Russia for another century.

The eighteenth century was a period of such degradation of the Church in Russia that she seemed past any hope of regeneration. Clerical training was in the hands of the Government, which cared nought for theologians but only for good officials. The traditional contempt for the parish priest increased, since he had been entrusted with police functions, and the wretched man was placed by the law on the last rung of the social ladder : until the end of the eighteenth century he was not exempt from corporal punishment, and the people could see their pastors publicly flogged for omitting some imperial title in the litanies or confusing the august personages whom one of the many palace revolutions had placed upon the steps of the throne.

Russians who flocked to Paris might have seen the Duchess of Berry, a daughter of France, deprived of Christian burial because of her scandalous life, or Louis XV refused the sacraments and forced to make public penance. . . . But they noticed nothing of this ; they only saw " court abbés " and harkened to Voltaire's gibes. Moreover, Russians could not conceive how a priest, or even a bishop, dared interfere with the private or public life of a person of rank or make the slightest protest against the flagrant immorality of the court.

Foreigners visiting Russia could scarcely believe themselves to be in a Christian country, but here they were as wrong as were Russians who saw France *only* as the kingdom of libertinage. In Russia, too, there existed currents of profound religious feeling, which sheltered in the monasteries.

Peter loathed monastic life, in which he rightly saw the expression of an ideal diametrically opposed to the one he wished to impose. He attempted to convert monasteries into hospitals or homes for disabled soldiers, but all his measures failed before the indomitable religious spirit entrenched in these ancient strongholds of the faith, where more than ever the ancient tradition of flight from a world doomed to perdition attracted thousands of souls.

The old Russian term for a religious vocation *spasat'sia* (save oneself) regained all its former significance, and monasteries found innumerable new vocations. And this in spite of the strict laws of Peter and his successors, forbidding acceptance of young men of military age, serfs without their masters' consent, artisans or merchants without a certificate from their place of registration, and so forth. These restrictions were meant to curtail religious vocations, which were viewed distrustfully by the Government because the inward life of the monasteries escaped State control and was a challenge to the " totalitarian " State with its minutely regulated *régime*. Yet monasteries could become a source of revenue, so the State crushed them under a fiscal system so heavy as to ruin them and make them unable to meet their obligations, especially the support of bishops and the synod. This served as a pretext for the Government of Catherine II (1764) to lay hands upon monastic lands, the upkeep of the despoiled monks being defrayed by the Government. This important reform has often been considered from a purely economic viewpoint as a fiscal measure : actually it had a deeper significance and aimed at bringing the religious down to a status of an employee similar to the parish priest.

Henceforth the number of monks, as that of the secular clergy, was strictly regulated. Monasteries and convents were divided into three " classes," according to the number of monks or nuns they were permitted to harbour, the Government allowing a modest sum for the upkeep of the " registered " religious. Final vows were permitted only subject to the assent of the Holy Synod, and the temporal power could not interfere at will with matters pertaining to monastic life. If until then it was able only to supervise the material side, now it could decide the exact number of religious, curtail them at its own discretion (there were monasteries of the third class with a right to twelve religious only !), impose various obligations, stressing that the monk was only a salaried official. Sooner or later the way would be clear for the total suppression of religious houses either as a heavy and useless burden upon the State or under some trumped-up pretext of the infringement of rules, and the legislation did actually give occasion for frequent infringements. Thus, in order to elude the law forbidding more monks than the " strength " (*shtat*) of each house allowed, fictitious registration in a monastery with a vacancy was recurred to. We see, for instance, Seraphim of Sarov entered in 1786 for his profession in the list of the monastery of Gorokhovo, whereas actually he never left the small house of Sarov to which subsequently he was to give such renown. Therefore the monasteries were ever under threat of accusation of some illegality.

It would have seemed that such oppression would contaminate monastic life with the secular spirit which had withered the rest of the country, but, on the contrary, the monasteries were the first to inaugurate a powerful religious reaction. At the end of the eighteenth century a great *staretz*, Paisiy Velichkovsky, was concerned in it. A native of the Ukraine who had spent most of his life at Mount Athos and in a Moldavian monastery, Paisiy never forgot the needs of the Russian monasteries, visiting them, exhorting them to return to the great patristic traditions, to fight ignorance and inertia. He started a movement to encourage religious studies, and again Russian monasteries returned to the mystical literature of the Eastern fathers. The great *staretz* was a tireless translator of Greek texts and founded a school of translation and interpretation ; thanks to him mystical theology flourished again on a basis of reliable documentation, and Russian monasteries paved the way for studies which, during the nineteenth century, were an honour to the four great ecclesiastical academies, especially a complete translation into Russian of the works of the Greek fathers. But Paisiy's influence was particularly felt in the internal organization of monastic life, most of the Russian monasteries accepting his system of " directors " chosen among the most revered monks, irrespective of their official status or office. This institution, whereby spiritual direction was freed from oppressive control, clerical or lay, quite naturally continued the old Russian tradition of the *startzy*—trustees of a sacred heritage. Thus in the nineteenth century monastic life was reclaimed under

F 2

the auspices of *startzy*, whose spiritual influence spread far beyond the enclosure of their monasteries, reaching the laity for whom the official Church had lost all prestige. But since bishops were recruited from the monks, inevitably the whole Church was quickened by the invigorating breadth of a renewed spirituality. So, as in all the most critical periods of Russian history, the monasteries again saved the faith and became a source of a new life for the Church.

Though outwardly the institutions were unchanged, the new spirit was transforming them from within. The full significance of a change, imperceptible at first, strongly marked in the last years of the nineteenth century, may be grasped if we study the currents outside the official Church which fed the religious feelings of the people and the intellectual classes, giving a new interpretation to ancient and well-nigh forgotten formulæ.

CHAPTER VI

THE RELIGION OF THE PEOPLE

WHEN schism broke the unity of the Russian Church great numbers of people remained outside her. The term *raskolnik* having always been rather indefinite, it is impossible to give even an approximate figure of their numbers. At the end of the last century the total figure for all sects was estimated at twenty millions, or about a quarter of the entire Russian population, racially and linguistically. This figure fluctuated greatly according to the broader or narrower application of the term *raskol* : sometimes it meant only the Old Believers, who issued from the seventeenth century schism, sometimes it designated the aggregate of all the sects formed during the last two centuries, some of which were of an origin alien to any Russian tradition. Baptists, however, who made great progress in the second half of the nineteenth century, were never included in this general term.

Nearly the entire rural population was in schism, and *raskol* had many adherents, not only in the upper classes, but also in the Tsar's palace : Peter the Great encountered enemies in his own family. But the new aristocracy and bureaucracy rallied to the official Church, which was so well adapted to the prevailing mood of religious indifference. The same can be said of Peter's other creations—the army and navy. Mass recruiting of soldiers for the Tsar's ceaseless campaigns tore young men from their homes, and made them an easy prey to any new-fangled idea, to contempt for all old traditions, even religious. The curious folklore of the time, composed in the barracks, pictures in its songs and tales this type of soldier and sailor as unprejudiced, irreverent, scoffing, fatalist, and daring. The worship of the Church was not neglected but followed with complex feelings, including love of beauty and an imperialist brand of patriotism.

A new social class was growing rapidly in numbers and importance : this was a middle class of artisans and small shopkeepers. Devoid of traditions, and anxious to maintain good relations with the civil authorities, they were docile to the official Church. It is possible that her predominance over the steadily growing multiple sects was maintained precisely owing to this uninterrupted accretion of the urban population and the influence it exercised over the peasants who drifted into the towns in quest of work.

These elements, constituting the bulk of the faithful of the synodal Church, represented social layers more susceptible to the influence of the secular spirit which was revolutionizing Russian thought and life. Loyalty to the Church was tantamount to loyalty to the Government and had nothing whatever to do with any religious convictions : on the contrary, it bore witness to a total indifference to the questions which had once so passionately interested the whole country. The Church had been transformed into a symbol of nationality : her banners were no longer an emblem of the Kingdom to come, but merely the colours of the earthly motherland. Such a banner was necessary, for Peter's new *régime* brought an influx of foreigners into Russia—soldiers, scientists, artists, workmen, merchants—who established colonies in the new capital and all over the country, enjoying every civic right and special privileges. They remained, nevertheless, foreigners, against whom national feeling sought to assert itself. Here the Church came to the rescue. It was through her that the gradual assimilation of alien elements was effected : mixed marriages, unheard of in old Muscovy, became common, and children born of such unions and baptized into the Russian Church became Russian by the very fact of their baptism ; later they assimilated the national mentality, even when their names indicated their foreign origin. Adherence to Orthodoxy was what mattered most, though it was only external, implying no convictions based upon any spiritual demands : it was just a proof of nationality.

For this new society the Church was nothing but an office where births, marriages, and deaths were registered, such civil acts being clothed with all the solemnity of an impressive rite. The Church also dispensed the treasure of her liturgy and chant, which never lost their hold upon Russians, so responsive to all artistic manifestations. But this response was superficial and did not derive from any intimate participation in the divine mysteries. Eucharistic worship never developed in Russia, the Mass had no greater significance than any other service : often solemn Vespers of the vigil of some great feast was better attended than Mass on the feast-day itself. These Vespers, followed by Matins, with their peculiarly beautiful singing, the Church an oasis of light in the midst of the surrounding darkness, the mystical spell of the night hours, had a greater attraction for Russians than Mass. We mention these features of Russian religious mentality because they were crystallizing at this time when the revolution of ideas and morals had loosened the bond uniting the Church and her children : all that survived was an æsthetic emotion and a certain respect for established authority.

If such was the spirit of the upper classes in so far

as they had not completely surrendered to agnosticism, the common people experienced their notion of the Church with more artlessness. As always, there existed a great disparity between outward worship, with its admixture of vague superstitions, and the coarseness of everyday life, with all its unconscious immorality, in spite of which there was the comfortable certainty of ultimate salvation because membership of the Church sufficed.

Now that the people could occasionally express this indifference to evil, they sometimes did so rather cynically. This is seen in the folklore of the time, especially in the famous *Povest o brazhnike* ("Tale of the Drunkard"), composed about the end of the seventeenth century or perhaps a few years later. It tells of the death of a hopeless drunkard whose soul came to the gates of Heaven. St. Peter forbids the drunkard to enter, who replies that, as he had never denied Christ, he had more right to Heaven than St. Peter. The drunkard is as insolent with other saints, and tells St. John that every sinner is entitled to divine forgiveness. The drunkard triumphs and enters Heaven with all the honours. This story is characteristic of the peculiar twist of mind of the unlettered people, among whom it originated and enjoyed a considerable success. So the Church's traditional tolerance for sin was bearing its fruit.

And now *raskol* was there to confront this tolerance

verging upon indifference and cynicism. We have
said that the actual causes of the great schism lay
beneath the superficial excitement aroused by the
revision of liturgical books ; we will examine one of
them. The healthier elements of the nation craved
for higher moral standards, thirsted for a life more in
conformity with the Christian ideal, as they understood it, and naturally these longings took the shape
of an idealization of the patriarchal past. This is
why danger was scented in any innovation, in every
attempt to introduce the smallest change into the
sacred heritage of the past. Exaggerated traditionalism grafted upon the grossest ignorance at
times assumed grotesque forms, but underlying this
was a moral force which constituted the power of
raskol proper, that is to say, those *raskolniks* known as
staroobryadtzy (Old Ritualists) and *starovyery* (Old
Believers).

Other sects sprang up, of a totally different spirit.
These made a clean break with old traditions and
sought to revive the idea of individual election and
the brotherhood of the elect gathered in small conventicles, a system which never fails to appeal to
those for whom a universal brotherhood of Christians seems too abstract an idea : they need to warm
themselves in close contact with others moved by the
same ideals. Such little tabernacles present many
dangers, for they encourage the arrogant delusion of

some special " election " through the principle
authority being substituted by the influence of a
irresponsible and ignorant head. With Russian
sectarians this quest of " the actual truth of God "
immediately assumed the most extravagant forms,
in which we may distinctly perceive two trends of
thought : one deriving from Protestantism, the
influence of which had been felt ever since the sixteenth century, the other due to dim mystical traditions of Eastern origin, traceable to the Gnostic and
Manichæan sects of the dawn of Christianity.

It is beyond the scope of this book to unravel the
skein of these many sects and examine their inter-
actions. They have defied any clear delimitations,
for rationalist sects, borrowing individualist notions,
were brought closer to the mystics,[1] who, in their
turn, often encroached upon the domain of traditionalism. This explains the confusion of the official
registers of the sects compiled by those who endeavoured to dispute with them.

The first to attempt a general refutation of their
errors was Dmitri, metropolitan of Rostov (+ 1709),
author of the famous *Rosysk* (Research concerning the
beliefs of *raskolniks*). Writing early in the eighteenth

[1] Both terms of " rationalists " and " mystics " have been accepted
by Russian and foreign writers to designate two groups of sects.
These terms are rather confusing, because there is as little rationalism in the one as true mysticism in the other group ; yet as these
terms have been sanctioned by usage, they are being retained in
the book. (Transl.)

century, only fifty years after the schism, he men-
tions twenty-nine different sects, some of which
disappeared from subsequent registers, whereas
others split into new groups which continued to
multiply uninterruptedly until the late nineteenth
century. We will follow the three main tendencies,
traditionalism, rationalism, mysticism, each of which
subdivided into two distinct currents, of which we
shall give a general idea.

Under *traditionalism* are to be understood the sects
which broke away from the Church in order to preserve the integrity of the sacred texts distorted by
revision. But, as we have said, the bulk of those
people knew these liturgical texts only by ear, a fact
which explains their attachment to each separate
word, each gesture, however insignificant. They
found arguments to support their case in the dim
memories of a distant past, antecedent to the time
when the Russian Church had taken a definite shape.
Thus an echo of former Christian unity is heard in
one of the absurd arguments advanced by *raskolniks*
against the "terrible" sin of shaving the beard : this
custom, they alleged, unknown to Christ and His
apostles, was introduced by a heretical (and imagin-
ary) Pope Peter the Stammerer. In a less absurd
form this survival of Roman memories expressed
itself in a legend which was very common among
raskolniks : Skazanie o byelom klobukye (Legend of the

White *Klobuk* [1]). The gist of it is that when the Empire was transferred from Rome to Byzantium Pope Sylvester sent his white *klobuk* to the Archbishop of Novgorod (another version corrected this anachronism, saying that the papal *klobuk* was brought to Novgorod at a later date). It is easy to trace this legend to the time when the conception of the " Third Rome " was being evolved, and it aimed at stressing Russia's independence from Constantinople. *Raskolniks* were wont to cite it when anxious to humble the Patriarch of Moscow and exalt the Archbishop of Novgorod. We may recall the fact that Novgorod, in close intercourse with the Latin West, was the cradle of heresies of a Western character; thus it became expedient to stress a Novgorodian filiation in order to undermine the authority of the innovators of Moscow and St. Petersburg, since Peter the Great was the centre of the official Church. This legend is also interesting as a proof that *raskol*, in spite of its strong national feeling, retained confused memories of the oneness of Christianity and especially of Rome's primacy, whereby the " Third Rome " was not the inheritor of Byzantine grievances but the heir appointed by Rome herself.

However, the influence of these vague reminis-

[1] *Klobuk* is a monk's cylindrical headgear covered with a long black veil, bishops, being monks, wear it too. By an ancient custom the *klobuk* of patriarchs and metropolitans is white.

cences upon the formation of *raskol* must not be exaggerated : they were but shapeless fragments emerging from the turmoil of ideas which fomented the rebellion against the official Church. What really mattered for this group of Old Believers was a blind loyalty to the agglomeration of traditions which they believed to represent the actual doctrine of the pre-Nikonian Church. This loyalty was put to a severe test when, in the second generation of *raskol*, death had taken away all schismatic bishops and priests, leaving the traditionalists without clergy, a critical situation which again led to dissensions.

Whilst there existed validly ordained priests the need for bishops was not felt, but the last surviving priests being unable to ordain others, every dodge, even simony, was resorted to in order to obtain ordinations by bishops of the official Church. There were also attempts to create a schismatic hierarchy of foreign origin.

The story of *raskol* is long and tragic, it is, in fact, the history of a considerable section of the Russian people during two centuries, and a section with a high standard of morals. Patriarchal customs, temperance, honesty were rewarded by material wealth ; the sober and hard-working *raskolniks* were the creators of Russia's industries and trade. In the new society which demanded energy and initiative they were the first to get rich, but their fortunes were put to the service of their sacred cause. Their wealth helped the Old Believers to weather all storms, to survive the persecutions of a jealous Church and distrustful Government. They had important establishments in St. Petersburg, and especially in Moscow, whose entire trade was in their hands, and they could afford to pay for concessions which legalized their existence. They also wielded great power in the interior of the country, the navigation on the Volga being owned by Old Believers as well as numerous commercial establishments along the river, some of which served as screens for churches and even monasteries.

But their exaggerated nationalism was in no wise tantamount to loyalty to the Imperial Government, which they judged by its foreign aspect, overlooking its great national achievements. Owing to this misconception they supported the rebellion of Pugatchev [1] in the reign of Catherine II, and also in 1812 sent delegates to welcome Napoleon upon his entry into Moscow. In the middle of the nineteenth century the Government took energetic steps to end this opposition : churches were closed, monasteries dissolved, and an attempt made to entice Old Believers into *edinovyerie* (" unity of faith "), whereby their priests would be subject to the jurisdiction of

[1] A Cossak who, pretending to be the murdered Tsar Peter III, headed a rebellion (1773–74) which assumed such proportions as to endanger the State. It was eventually suppressed by armed force. (Transl.)

the bishops of the synodal Church. This was rejected by the great majority, and the struggle went on until the early years of this century, when, religious tolerance being proclaimed, Old Believers were at last able to legalize their Church. A few years later the revolution, with its terrible religious persecutions, brought martyrdom to Old Believers as well as to their former enemies.

We have said that dissensions over the problem of a hierarchy had resulted in a rupture within the traditionalist section of Old Believers. As early as the beginning of the eighteenth century there were *bezpopovtzi* ("priestless" ones) who, denying the validity of the ordinations by Nikonian bishops, preferred to do without any clergy at all. These dissidents broke up into a number of bodies, many of which closely resembled the rationalist sects. On one essential point, however, they widely differed. Though they refused to obey a hierarchy tainted with Nikonian heresy, they admitted the hierarchical principle as taught by the Church ; they considered that, since fortuitous circumstances had deprived them of their clergy, they had to recur to expediency. Laymen being allowed to administer Baptism *in extremis*, *bezpopovtzi*, in order to manifest their loyalty to the Church, maintained this usage, but with the disappearance of a priesthood they lost the Eucharist. Soon the custom of having small private chapels spread among them, and their families prayed together under the direction of an " elder." But these *bezpopovtzi*, who acknowledged the hierarchy and sacraments *in principle*, retained the veneration of saints, and most of their ritual observances were, theologically considered, very similar to the Old Believers, with whom they were usually confused under the general appellation of *raskolniks*. The *bezpopovtzi* split into a number of sects : some retained their close connection with the Old Believers, others drifted towards rationalism ; there were also groups inspired by a messianism which closely allied them to mystical sectarianism. Thus *bezpopovtzi* were an intermediate link between traditionalism and the two other tendencies, rationalist and mystical.

The origin of the *rationalist* sects is easily traced to the Novgorodian heresies of the fifteenth and sixteenth centuries which the secular power, urged by Joseph Volokolamsky, determined to destroy. The *Judaizers* promptly disappeared and were no more heard of until the great schism, when both *Strigolniki* and *Judaizers* suddenly re-emerged into the limelight. At first they were confused with the general mass of *raskolniks*, but later they appeared independently among the sects which had definitely severed all connection with ancient traditions. This shows that rationalist tendencies had survived among those sections of the people which were not under any ecclesiastical influence. There are indications of a secret and uninterrupted intercourse between these *Judaizers* and the Lithuanian and Polish sects issuing from the Protestant Reformation, particularly the *Socinians*. Until the schism such tendencies had remained latent, but when, following upon the great disruption, *raskol* itself broke up into a number of sects, it was found that some of them had nothing whatsoever in common with the Old Believers. These, as two centuries earlier, were called " Jewish " or "Iconoclasts" because they rejected the sacraments of the Church, the veneration of saints, and all outward observances, including fasting. This latter peculiarity was the dominant trait of the sect of *molokane* (from *moloko*—milk), a name given because of their neglect of the rule of abstinence from all dairy produce during Lent. But this general name of *molokane* covered a number of different sects. Some of them were known as *subbotniki* ("sabbatarians" —from *subbota*—sabbath), because of their keeping the Sabbath (*i.e.*, Saturday) in preference to Sunday. The teaching of these sects is based principally upon the Old Testament, and their services consisted of the singing of psalms and hymns of their own composition. They deny the Incarnation, but appear to have retained some of the dogmas of the Church, though they interpret them allegorically.

In the eighteenth century these sects did not number many adherents : occasionally their conventicles could be discovered lost among the overwhelming masses of dissidents of every kind, the majority of whom belonged to the mystical sects more attuned to the Russian soul. The cruel persecutions of Peter and his successors promoted a reaction which took the shape of a fanatical mysticism deepened by the spectacle of upper-class irreligion : it was natural that the people inclined more towards an apocalyptic trend of thought and the uncontrolled mysticism which suited them better than a rather drab rationalism. The progress of the rationalist sects started in the early nineteenth century and continued steadily to our days : it was primarily due to the spread of education, strongly secular in character and unfavourable to any transcendentalism. Another factor was the dissemination of the pietistical writings of Russian freemasons and of the Bible published in the vernacular by the Bible Society which settled in Russia under Alexander I. This was another means of fighting the State Church, which was participating in the mystical renaissance inaugurated among the upper classes.

But the chief factor in the advance of the rationalist sects was the influence of German settlers who, under Catherine II, established themselves in the region of the Volga, whence they spread all over

South Russia. Some were Lutherans, others Catholics, but the majority were Mennonites, whose active proselytizing had in the second half of the nineteenth century won over a considerable part of the Ukraine. The prosperity of these settlers, envied by the Russian peasants, was due to superior agricultural methods and tools, and the State granted them such privileges as the exemption of conscientious objectors from military service. This exemption, however, not including Russian converts, the latter naturally nursed a grievance, which at times led to conflicts with the authorities. The Government, to rid itself of some of the *molokane*, transported them to Transcaucasia. Fifty years later the *Dukhobory* ("Spirit-wrestlers"), a sect closely related to the Mennonites, quarrelled with the Government upon the subject of conscientious objection, and emigrated to Canada, actively helped by Tolstoy. The State was now as powerless to crush the progress of these sects as was the Church, whose " lay missionaries," enlisted from among synodal officials, were looked upon with open contempt. The Mennonites, however, were able to carry on their propaganda very successfully. They paid good wages to their labourers, gave them plentiful food, meat and milk being served on all abstinence days, and the only thing they demanded in return was the banishing of all icons from their houses.

This paved the way for the advent of the *Baptists* in the middle years of the nineteenth century under the name of *Stunda* (German *Stunde*—hour, from special hours of devotion). They made rapid progress. Again under this new name were included several sects : Baptists properly speaking, Evangelical Christians, and such small groups as Adventists, New Israelities, and others. At the outbreak of the revolution this sectarian movement was very powerful : it had lost every vestige of a national character, and was closely related to the German and English bodies which directed it. Protestant influences were strong in the region of the lower Volga, parts of the Caucasus, and the Ukraine, as well as in the larger cities, where they sometimes mingled with *bezpopovtzi* of rationalist tendencies. If a denominational map of pre-revolutionary Russia were drawn, one might, roughly, mark Protestant and rationalist sects in the south, *bezpopovtzi* in the north ; Moscow would be the stronghold of Old Believers, who also dominated the old cities along the upper Volga, and through the middle Volga spread to Siberia, where they formed important groups. Such a delimitation is, however, only approximate, for everywhere there was meeting and mingling of sects of a widely diverging spirit, and the industrial progress and home colonization of the nineteenth century had greatly modified the life of the people and occasioned frequent re-groupings.

But not all Protestant sects were rationalist : next to the strictly Puritan groups there were others influenced by Protestant *mysticism*, with its exaltation of individual aspiration and its revivalist gatherings. When in the eighteenth century an attempt was made to classify sects of foreign origin they were all registered as *Quakers*, together with the sects whose national mysticism derived from very ancient Eastern traditions.

In our geographical distribution mystical sects are omitted because they cannot be localized. Mysticism of a kind permeated all the groups, it was a kind of no-man's land where all dissidents met, and it was also found in the domain of the State Church. Russian religion was full of a mystical spirit which, at times, assuming a concrete shape, showed the definite contours of some particular sect. But more often this was impossible because the sectarians given to strange practices were in no wise anxious to organize themselves into distinct groups. On the contrary, they pretended to adhere to some known sect or, more often, to the official Church, whose observances they kept : this is the reason why the actual number of sectarians in Russia has remained unknown. Statistics compiled shortly before the revolution put their number at about twenty-five per cent. of the entire population, but such figures are inadequate, for about half of the people registered as belonging to the State Church were actually either secretly affiliated to some obscure sect or strongly influenced by its ideology. The reception of Holy Communion did not interfere with the secret practices of an hysterical, and often morbid, mysticism.

Even in its beginnings Russian Christianity showed signs of a Manichæan dualism, a turmoil of ideas which, in so far as they could be disciplined by the Church, became the power of Russian monasticism. But the flood of these ideas transcended orthodox limits and joined the great stream of Eastern heresies which included the Byzantine *Paulicians* and the Bulgarian *Bogomiles* with their Western offshoot— the *Catharists*. Old chronicles mention the presence in Kiev in the early eleventh century of isolated heretics of the *bogomile* type. They were soon lost in the mass of the faithful who obeyed the Church. Such a conflict as the great struggle against the Albigensians could never have occurred in Russia, where the doctrine of the Church lacked any theological precision and exterior observances were more important than the profession of dogmatic truth.

There were many disorderly elements in the old Muscovite Church. *Yurodivye*, wandering about the streets, followed by a respectful crowd harkening to their ravings ; pilgrims who did nothing but tramp from shrine to shrine ; " whirling " monks ; *klikoo-*

shas, or hysterical women, who cried out in church ; " prophets " appearing from nowhere, who sometimes incurred punishment when their pronouncements took a political turn : all these neurotic people, refractory to any discipline, shared a common belief in an individual inspiration in the matter of faith and a contempt for work and all social order. These views were stimulated by vague dualist doctrines, wherein the family and social duties were seen as pertaining to a materialistic and corrupt world as opposed to the freedom of the " higher life."

This mystical movement was at first confused with the *raskol* in general, and it is difficult to distinguish the part played by its followers in the violent resistance of the first dissenters in the face of persecution. For instance, when Peter's savage methods provoked collective suicide by burning, the Old Believers are considered to have been the voluntary victims of these holocausts : the traditionalist *raskol* claims as its martyrs the scores of thousands who went to their death in companies, clothed in long white tunics, singing hymns within the timber enclosure which was then set on fire. Cases are known when some two thousand people—men, women, and children— submitted to this voluntary *auto-da-fe !* It would seem that such collective madness was not due to the Old Believers, since they were characterized by balanced and practical minds, whereas suicide by burning or by burying alive was a feature of the " mystical " sects down to our own times. A trial which took place some twenty years before the revolution revealed that nine fanatics from the neighbourhood of Odessa, in order to escape from a doomed world, had themselves buried alive. In our opinion, then, suicide by burning, so usual among the first dissidents, did not originate in the *raskol* proper.

Only in the second half of the eighteenth century did the different sects begin to be defined and, Peter III having revoked the persecuting laws, were able to organize. This is why the miserable husband of Catherine II became so dear to *raskolniks* that Pugatchev, who assumed his name, enlisted their support in his rebellion which shook Catherine's throne. It was also with the name of Peter III that *Khlysty* and other false mystical sects linked their traditions. Those sects manifested two tendencies : the followers of one were anxious to spread their tenets among the upper classes, and displayed respect for the State Church ; the other would have nothing to do with the world's affairs and hid among the people. Occasionally they might be distinguished by some peculiar or grotesque practice : thus the *Dyrkovtzy* (*dyra*—hole) bored a hole in the wall of their cottage and prayed before it : a crude symbol for the idea of spirit breaking its way to freedom through matter. Another sect, the *Byeguny* (runners) had no fixed abode ; the earth being only a place of exile, men were pilgrims ; these people were also known as *Stranniki* (wanderers), for on their endless journeyings they often joined a group of pilgrims on the way to some shrine. Thus the line of demarcation was here, as so often, scarcely perceptible, for these sects were closely connected with the popular anarchical and nomad spirit so specifically Russian.

It is impossible to describe the various forms this so-called mysticism assumed, fluctuating between heresy and orthodoxy, with a strong flavour of dualism.

The *Khlysty* are the best exponents of the trend, and they played a prominent part in the religious destinies of Russia. Undoubtedly they descend from the Manichæans of the old Slavonic world. The origin of their name is uncertain : some believe it to be a deformation of the name of Christ, others think that *khlyst* (whip) is an allusion to the flagellation whereby they brought on a state of delirium. Their theological system bore traces of the old conception of two primordial principles, the material world being the creation of the principle of evil. The condemnation of matter in the case of one group was absolute, hence the independent sect of *skoptzy* (*castrati*), who exacted this voluntary mutilation from their adepts. Among the *khlysty* proper their negation of the material world manifested itself in complete contempt for its laws : as they had no compulsory moral code there was no such thing as sin ; certain ascetical practices were urged in order to attain to a sort of ecstasy wherein the gift of tongues and prophecy was claimed. In order to reach this state at their secret meetings they danced together in a circle or whirled separately (like the so-called dancing Dervishes) to the singing of hymns and cries for the descent of the spirit.

Sometimes the whirl was replaced by jumping (hence the name *pryguny*—jumpers). The meetings of this sect were the occasion of much licentiousness of the kinds known to the student of the morbid phenomena of religious fanaticism. *Khlysty* are known to have occasionally indulged in such excesses, a fact which led to their inclusion among the immoral and dangerous sects forbidden by law. However, this was only a casual occurrence, and the " twelve commandments " of their alleged founder were of an ascetic kind.

These " twelve commandments " started by the claim of their author, Danilo Filippovitch, to be the Messiah. This strange person lived in the time of the great schism : he showed his contempt for the whole thing by ordering his followers to throw all books, old and new, into the river : they were useless, he said, for the new revelation was written in the heart. This man was the follower of a certain Kapiton, said to have been a friend of Tsar Michael : curiously, a sect owing its origins to this Kapiton was known in the eighteenth century under the name of *Cupidons* (Cupids !), which shows the ignorance of the new Russian society of the tradition of its own past. With Peter the Great, Russia took a leap from the Middle Ages into a modern world, but the survivals of mediæval mentality were disconcertingly tenacious and blended curiously with the new ideas.

The *khlysty* were singular in that, whilst keeping in touch with the illiterate masses, they kept an eye upon the intellectual classes, striving to safeguard them from agnosticism, and often succeeding in gaining influence over them. Danilo Filippovitch had followers in all social classes, and is considered the founder of the modern *khlysty* because he gave a certain organization to the shapeless sect. Each separate group was known as a *korabl* (ship)—an allusion to Noah's ark or to a ship sailing on stormy seas. A woman headed each of these ships under the name of *bogoroditza* (mother of God) ; her spiritual son was a " *khristos*," surrounded by twelve apostles. Such an organization obtained to our days, with " messiahs " appearing in every generation, usually appointed by the *bogoroditza*. As for Danilo Filippovitch, he was declared to have been the incarnation of the Lord God Sabaoth, who, after consolidating his work on earth, returned to Heaven in a fiery chariot.

The " ships " navigated Moscow and St. Petersburg, where they enlisted many followers among intellectuals and illiterate, aristocracy and clergy. Suslov, follower of Danilo Filippovitch, living in Moscow with his *bogoroditza* and twelve apostles, had a fervent disciple in a Prince Meschersky, who was connected with the greatest Russian families, even the imperial. Another famous *khlyst*, Lupkin, and his son Seraphim, a *hieromonk* (priest-monk), spread the teaching among the Moscow clergy, especially in the women's convents : a nun, Nastasia Karpovna, played the part of *bogoroditza*, meetings taking place in one of the larger nunneries. These meetings were denounced on moral grounds. A trial followed, ending in a conviction, and Nastasia Karpovna was beheaded in St. Petersburg in 1737. The *khlysty* became more wary, and the " ships " incurred no more charges of immorality, but they continued to organize in both capitals. They were always under powerful protection, and, moreover, their followers were careful not to advertise their sectarianism, but to conform to the observances of the State religion.

The disciples of Lupkin and his wife, Akulina, having disagreed, the latter became *bogoroditza* of another important group, among whom the celebrated Kondraty Selivanov, founder of the *skoptzy*, arose. Their practice of self-mutilation excepted, *skoptzy* were similar to the *khlysty*. Selivanov was arrested for his propaganda, punished by the *knut*, and deported to Irkutsk. There he impersonated Tsar Peter III, so beloved of *raskolniki*. The legend that the Emperor had been the actual founder of this sect spread rapidly, but Kondraty lived unmolested when the authorities saw that no political significance attached to this name. The closing years of the eighteenth century saw him again in St. Petersburg. According to one legend, Paul I had sent for him. The Emperor treated him kindly, but had him placed under supervision in an asylum, where Alexander I visited him in 1802, had a long talk with him and ordered his liberation : this was the beginning of the astounding career of this neurotic peasant. Living in the houses of wealthy merchants belonging to his sect, Kondraty presided over meetings to which flocked many important people. He numbered among his patrons Prince Galitzin, procurator of the Holy Synod, subsequently minister for public education, and a personal friend of the Tsar. Prince Kochubey, minister for the interior, shielded Selivanov and his followers, whose numbers rapidly increased to three or four thousand in the capital alone, many adepts belonging to the imperial guards.

Success went to Kondraty's head. One of his

followers was a Polish nobleman Elensky, at one time chamberlain to King Stanislaus Poniatowsky, and who lived in St. Petersburg in the Alexandro-Nevsky laura (monastery). Under Kondraty's influence this nobleman laid before Tsar Alexander a scheme of a " theocratic constitution " of the empire whereby *khlysty* and *skoptzy* would be the sovereign's official advisers, guiding him by their revelations of the divine will. This was going too far, and Elensky was declared insane and confined to a monastery in Suzdal, where he lost no time in organizing a " ship " among nuns of a neighbouring convent, one of whom became a much revered *bogoroditza*. Kondraty's own position remained unchanged, and, in spite of his advanced age, he continued for a few more years to be the idol of society people in quest of new sensation.

Cases of self-mutilation having occurred among officers of the guards, the Government thought it time to take measures against *skoptzy*. Kondraty Selivanov was exiled to the same monastery as Elensky, where he ended his days in peace, and nothing more was heard of the " White pigeons " (another name for the *skoptzy*). The only memory which survived was the legend that Paul I belonged to the sect. But the *khlysty*, their " ships," their meetings and dances and prophetesses, continued to enjoy a great vogue. One of the admirers of old

Kondraty organized a " ship " in her own home : this lady was a Baroness Buxhoevden, widow of a Colonel Tatarinov. Her mother having had a post at court, she lived in one of the imperial palaces, and there she whirled rapturously with her friends, among whom we meet again Prince Galitzin, with Baron Buxhoevden, brother of the prophetess, and many other distinguished people. Alexander I listened respectfully to the " inspired " pronouncements of Mme. Tatarinova.

All this madness seemed to disappear in the reign of Nicholas I, a martinet full of strong commonsense. *Khlysty* went into hiding : yet the secret filiation of their " ships " was never broken, nor was the idea that their sect was called to a spiritual government of the State forgotten. The coronation in the Caucasus in 1857 of a *khlyst* called Maxim Rudometkin, a happening insufficiently elucidated, seems to have had something to do with this curious notion. About the end of last century *khlysty* suddenly reappeared in the capital. A " ship " steered by a Daria Smirnova in a suburb of St. Petersburg attracted a crowd of devotees, the bulk of whom belonged to the middle class. *Bogoroditza* Daria Smirnova was tried for some infringement of the law, and expelled from the capital a year or two before the Great War : she had numbered the notorious Rasputin among her friends.

The part played by this man in the pre-revolutionary years is better understood when seen in the light of the long tradition which inspired him. For well over a century the waves of popular " mysticism " had played around the steps of the throne : it was the connecting link between the upper classes and the vague aspirations of the people ; the intellectuals imbued by the secular spirit remained outside. This disorderly tendency was believed to be the true expression of national feelings, and it satisfied the religious needs which the official Church did not know how to meet.

Indeed, the ritual of the Church was merely a screen concealing a varied assortment of religious ideas which no authority kept together. Excesses of sectarian fanaticism, when too glaringly opposed to the ideal of a national religion, were repressed by the State. But the Church was powerless to formulate this ideal : all through the centuries she had lived as the national religion, but now the religious idea had developed independently, whilst the national idea had flooded over its former boundaries. The Russian mind had been troubled first by the great schism, and a century later by a great social reconstruction. Now moral and intellectual restoration had become the urgent problem. Russian consciousness called for a broad synthesis, and it was the lay minds, not the Church, which went in quest of it.

CHAPTER VII

NATIONAL PHILOSOPHY

THE irreligion which from the early eighteenth century had affected the Russian upper classes was not, as in Western Europe, the outcome of a ratiocinated atheist trend of thought, but rather a violent reaction against all the ideas which had hitherto governed social and domestic life. Russian society had never gone through the philosophical crisis of the Renaissance, had not experienced a gradual process of de-Christianization, and the change in its mentality was due not to some new conception of life, but to the fact that the old ideological foundation had been shaken by the break-up of morals and of the whole social structure. New social forms having been adopted wholesale, it followed that the entire traditional mentality was thereby rejected. The Russian, clean-shaven and rigged out after the latest Paris fashion, was confident that he had severed every link with the past; his wife, too, dancing powdered and *decolletée* at every ball, was intoxicated with the new world

98

which had set her free from the rigid Muscovite seclusion.[1]

To moral relaxation corresponded an intellectual libertinage indulged in with all the gusto of a school-boy discovering a new and, as he thinks, better world. This society dated the beginning of its era with Peter the Great, and would know nought of any earlier past ; the literature of the time spoke of Peter as the creator, the father, of Russia. When under Catherine II higher education did actually make great progress, and not fashions only but ideas also were being imported from Paris, Russian society believed it was experiencing a spiritual rebirth, as a contemporary poet wrote : " Peter gave us bodies, Catherine has given us souls."

But the break with the past was far less complete than was imagined. The first brief spell of irreligion passed, obscure survivals came again to the surface, not always understood, yet strong enough to link the new mentality with that of the old Moscow. People realized that they did have a past, that their balance had been lost and that in order to stabilize this new society it was necessary to establish it upon a foundation composed of old fragments re-adapted to new demands. Political expansion accelerated this re-construction. Peter's reforms resulted in the creation

[1] This " purdah " of the Russian woman was the result of Tartar influence ; her liberation was the work of Peter. (Transl.)

of a formidable military power which in the eighteenth century successively crushed all Russia's traditional enemies, Sweden, Poland, and Turkey. Catherine II achieved the annihilation of Poland, the conquest of the Black Sea coast, and the destruction of Turkey's might. At long last the Cross had triumphed over the Crescent, and the time seemed near when it would again shine above the dome of Hagia Sophia at Constantinople. This prospect revived the consciousness of Russia's historical and religious mission and the Muscovite dream of the "Third Rome." Scholars began to study history, their researches paving the way for Karamzin's celebrated *History of the Russian State*, published at the beginning of the nineteenth century, and written in a spirit of *non ad narrandum, sed ad probandum*. The Russian mind had reverted to its ancient traditions which showed it a goal to attain, a mission to fulfil. The goal was the "gathering of the Russian land," with the addition of the heritage of Byzantium, the mission—the exaltation of the Orthodox Cross not over the Turkish Crescent only, but above the whole world. Old Muscovy's patriotism had been predominantly religious, so the new Russian imperialism was directed towards a religious regeneration.

For a long time such aspirations were not fully grasped, they ripened slowly, and the result of their subconscious working manifested itself considerably later. The distinctive trait of the Russian mind in the eighteenth century is incoherence, due to the shock of conflicting tendencies. Even under Peter and his immediate successors revolting irreverence somehow co-existed with a respect for the outward forms of worship, and the passing of time only strengthened this external religion, which became the expression of a national pride. Under Catherine, Russian society no longer indulged in a servile aping of the West : proud of its successes, it gloried in being a world apart, though this particularism could not become a narrow nationalism, because at this very time the ruling class was assimilating the foreign elements which had flocked into the country Thus religion was the only distinctive feature to justify pretentions to an exalted historical mission—it formed a link with the past, which in its turn lent it stability.

Foreigners overlooked this reconstitution of a religious mentality : they made a mistake (as did also many historians of a later date) in imagining that in Catherine's time Russian society was indifferent to religion, strongly imbued with " Voltairianism," whereas this was only a passing and superficial aspect. A great personage was quite capable of flaunting his agnosticism for the edification of foreigners, whilst professing very different views in his home and before his deeply religious peasants.

It has to be remembered that the cultured class of Russia was exclusively constituted of landowners, who never lost touch with the soil, and this obtained until the later years of the last century. Whilst the world of Versailles had been completely severed from the peasantry, and had fallen under the spell of " philosophical " urban theorisers, Russia had no middle class, her gentry were the only educated element, and they were firmly rooted in a soil where religion, if often distorted, was still vigorous. This explains the influence popular sectarianism occasionally exercised upon higher society. If some noblemen were dominated by *khlysty* and *yurodivye*, it was only because under the thin veneer of French education their mentality did not differ sensibly from the people's.

For a country squire living on his land far away from the capital these affinities were more strongly marked, because he had gradually shed the ideas and manners acquired at school or in his regiment and had reverted to type, with all its traditional superstitions and religious nationalism. This class of country squire, together with the *starovyer* merchant and the peasant masses with their sectarian bias, constituted the real Russia, which was not reflected in the Petersburg " salons " or in the correspondence of Catherine with Grimm and Voltaire.

Moreover, the influx of foreign notions was not necessarily in conflict with " mystical " tendencies. Initiation to European thought was also an initiation to German philosophy, with its strong theological bent. Skovoroda, Russia's first philosopher (1722–1794), had studied under Wolf and had imported from Germany a mixture of pietism and anarchical individualism which, grafted upon the classical education he had received in the Kiev Academy, made him one of the most original thinkers of his time. In many ways he was a forerunner and the first of the list of the great inquiring intellects which in the next century were to adorn Russia. An indefatigable seeker after truth, simultaneously pantheist and Christian, loving the liturgy whilst refusing any obedience to the State Church, often incoherent, though always sincere, an enthusiast of poverty and humility, believing himself called to preach them, Skovoroda resigned his professorship and spent the remainder of his life tramping South Russia dressed as a peasant and living upon charity. This first Russian " intellectual " is a compromise between the Europeanized cultured class and the people which gave birth to *yurodivye* and surrounded them with veneration, a hyphen connecting the divergent social layers which had not yet found their bearings.

In the circles where Western influence pre-

dominated, new "mystical" currents revealed themselves, and these were linked with freemasonry. We
are not concerned with the political side of the net-
work of secret societies in Western Europe, which
also played a revolutionary part in Russia, where
masonic lodges rapidly increased : what interests us
here is that Russian freemasonry laid a particular
stress upon the mystical aspect of a secret teaching
closely connected with the Rosicrucians, the Illu-
minati, and Martinists. What is still more significant
is the fact that Illuminism insinuated itself into the
conventicles which harboured *khlysty* "ships." In
the middle of the eighteenth century Kolesnikov, a
well-known *khlyst* personally known at court, was
given the surname of Masonov, because of his
intimate relations with freemasonry. The writings
of German mystics, especially those of Yung, Stilling,
and Eckartshausen, enjoyed a considerable and last-
ing vogue : translations of their works spread among
the lower classes and gave a new impetus to rationalist sectarianism, grounded upon an uncontrolled
interpretation of the Bible. In the upper class Boehme,
Swedenborg, and especially Saint-Martin, were
chief favourites, and the last-named's *Des erreurs et de
la vérité* became the Bible of Russian intellectuals :
after Novikov's private press had issued a first
edition, the book underwent innumerable reprints
and adaptations. Martinists, under the leadership

of Novikov and subsequently of his friend Senator Lopukhin, exercised a paramount influence upon the intellectual life of Russia until the early years of the nineteenth century. This group satisfied souls hungering for mystical experience outside the bounds of the State Church.

Echoes of the revolution in France violently interrupted these reveries of the mystical brotherhood. The Government became suspicious of them, and even Martinists incurred Catherine's wrath : repressions, however, were but a passing storm, for Jacobinism, evolving into a militant atheism, became the chief enemy. Mystical societies were again treated leniently, and they enjoyed the patronage of Alexander I until the last years of his reign, when the political aims of freemasonry were revealed. The Russian mind was also being profoundly impressed by a very different trend of Western thought : it had at last discovered the Catholic ideology. The Catholic Church had been a closed book, Rome being a hostile power in alliance with all Russia's enemies, and, her Europeanization coinciding with a triumph of free thought, Russia received a civilization seemingly lacking all memories of a dead mediæval past. So her surprise was great when she became aware of the fact that " papism " was in no wise a political party but the foundation of a deep and universal conception of religion, and that its theology implied a philosophy of history.

This discovery was gradual : at first Russians learnt to know the Jesuits, whom Catherine patronized to spite the Holy See, which had dissolved the Society—the excellence of their schools was recognized and the sons of the best families attended them. The coming of French refugees revealed another unexpected fact—the brilliant French society, credited with agnosticism, was seen to possess another religious aspect. The drawing-rooms of St. Petersburg re-echoed to the voice of Joseph de Maistre, there were some sensational conversions, and an intellectual effort was made to understand this new world which did not fit in at all with the national religious traditions : but eventually these last prevailed.

National pride, intensified by political expansion, was again reverting to the imperialist messianism of the " Third Rome." That Russia's religious past had been but one long misunderstanding was inadmissible, for it was realized that this newly re-discovered past would constitute a stable basis for the imperialist dream which, through the mists of Catherine's " Greek plan," visualized the cupolas of Hagia Sophia, the restoration of the Eastern Empire in a new splendour, the fulfilment of a great mission. But this mission demanded the maintenance of the religious particularism which alone gave it a meaning. There was a violent nationalist reaction, which found expression in contemporary literature against the slavish copying of Western Europe ; this exaggerated nationalism was also resolutely opposed to the infiltration of Catholic ideas, all the more dangerous because so disconcerting. The new imperialism had not yet discovered its precise definition, but it could be foreseen that it would be a negation of Rome's historical mission : thus the hostility towards Rome was resurrected. Conversions to Catholicism were hindered by public opinion far more than by any legal prohibitions.

This conflict of ideas was further complicated by the wave of patriotism which swept over the land in the time of the Napoleonic wars : the disasters of Austerlitz and Friedland came as a great shock to Russians, convinced, as they were, of their invincibility ; then followed the epic of 1812, the repulse of the invader, the victorious march through Europe, the Russian army's entrance into Paris with its Tsar in the *rôle* of arbiter of the world. Such splendid success seemed to justify the most exaggerated hopes, and Russians felt the time had come to define the philosophy of their own history.

It has often been said that the sojourn of the Russian army in France accelerated the revolutionary movement in Russia, because the young officers imported ideas which a decade later led to the military "Decembrist" rising. This opinion narrows the scope of the problem which confronted the Russian mind when it encountered a Europe refreshed by the revolutionary storm. Russia had known all about Jacobinism from its very beginnings, and there was no need to go as far as Paris in order to read the Declaration of the Rights of Man ; moreover, for half a century Russia had harboured subversive secret societies. A point which interests us and has been overlooked is that these officers, representing the only cultured class in Russia, saw Catholic France emerging from her ruin, and came to know about her mediæval antecedents, which revealed themselves as a strong and active factor of European psychology. They were able to appreciate the value of the Catholic ideology, which had moulded Europe's social structure and which, in this quest for a new social order, now reappeared again ; so their philosophy of history assumed a quite unexpected aspect.

In Western Europe the ideological rehabilitation of the Middle Ages took the shape of what is called "romanticism." This movement first reached Russia through the ballads of Schiller in Zhukovsky's masterly rendering, and the novels of Walter Scott, which enjoyed an enduring vogue. But this romantic literature could not deeply affect the Russian mind because it knew nothing of the Middle Ages, and so in its literature romanticism manifested itself chiefly under the form of Byronic acute individualism. In order to grasp the full significance of the clashing ideas which were shaking Europe at the time of the Bourbon restoration, it was imperative to know something of her past history and understand the meaning of this conflict between mediæval traditions and those of the Renaissance and the eighteenth century. This was achieved by one of the Russian officers who had witnessed the restoration in France ; his name was Tchaadaev.

In reading him it is easy to recognize his indebtedness to those Western writers who had attempted to elaborate a philosophy of history in the light of current events. Tchaadaev had frequented the drawing-rooms of St. Petersburg in the days of Joseph de Maistre and had certainly read his *Du Pape ;* he also knew Chateaubriand and Bonald. But his great originality lay in that he had the audacity to apply to Russia considerations provoked by the sight of Europe where, in spite of so many vicissitudes, the influence of the past was yet so strong. Russia clung to her national religion because she believed it to be the symbol of her political existence ; Tchaadaev perceived that Europe, too, had lived by a religious ideal, which had impregnated her thought, and that this ideal, being universal, soared far above any national rivalries and could therefore defy the passing and changes of time. History was the realization of an idea in the world, and only such human groupings as were inspired by an idea were entitled to a place in it.

This conception of history as a manifestation of a transcending idea was borrowed by Tchaadaev from Schelling, whom he had known personally. Schelling's philosophy had reached Russia, and was being passionately studied by young intellectuals, who more than ever hung on to German philosophy because of the distrust they now felt for anything hailing from France, though the francophobia of 1812 had given way to an indifferent contempt for a France now shorn of all her power. For those who had never understood the historical and religious evolution of Western thought, it was still more difficult to detect the return to traditions anterior to the " philosophism " of the eighteenth century : viewed from this particular angle the restoration seemed to be a last convulsion amidst a chaos of ruin. Young Russia looked to Germany as the strongest intellectual centre, and Schelling's philosophy, with its " universal spirit " manifested in history, seemed to supply an answer to those who sought some meaning in Russia's historical evolution. Nevertheless, when interest in German thought was at its highest, these Russian seekers overlooked the " back to the Middle

Ages " movement which had drawn Novalis and his group of romantic idealists towards Catholicism. Russia knew Germany as a Protestant country only, and any Catholic renaissance there seemed to her stranger and more disconcerting even than one in France. She had now a conception of Western Europe, wherein Latin countries were degenerate, whilst Germany and England, purged of the Latin *virus*, preserved their intellectual powers in full. Thus the traditional dislike of Catholicism was translated from the domain of religion into that of philosophy and sociology. It was upon this ground that Tchaadaev openly attacked anti-Catholicism. He declared that Catholicism had been and ever would be the only vital force in Europe, the pivot of her history, and that a country which had remained outside the great Roman unity had forfeited the right to an existence deserving of any notice.

At first Tchaadaev voiced his opinions in private only ; later he expressed them in a French correspondence which for some years circulated in manuscript among his friends ; finally, in 1836, he issued a Russian translation of the first of these *Lettres philosophiques* in a Moscow periodical.

It came as a bombshell and was viewed as an abominable attack upon Russia's dearest and most sacred ideals. Indeed, the writer, dismissing

Russia's past and present, pronounced her to be isolated and useless because she had remained outside the great Christian development headed by Rome, because religious stagnation had led to intellectual sterility, to a lack of social organization, to moral impotence. The picture was painted too black. But it was not the sarcastic tone, very common in the literature of the day, which aroused such general indignation, but the repudiation of a glorious past, the direct attack upon the ideal of a national religion which was the basis of Russian consciousness. Tchaadaev was declared insane by imperial decree and subjected for a year to medical and police supervision : he was also forbidden ever to publish his writings again.

As in many other cases, Tchaadaev's conversion to Catholicism would have passed unnoticed : it was the fact that he viewed Russian history from a Catholic angle which appeared so crazy, his bitter criticism of a religious particularism in which national pride gloried. A curious thing has to be noted : at no time was this affair considered to involve any question of faith or dogmatic principles ; Tchaadaev's philosophical conception was a secular heresy, a crime of *lèse-nation :* that is why it seemed so unbearable. In the opposition to Tchaadaev's thesis, Russia at last found the needed formula for her philosophy of history ; his considerations upon Europe's Catholic rebirth led to this unforeseen result and helped on the crystallization of doctrines diametrically opposed to his own.

Ironically enough, the revolutionary elements, hateful to Tchaadaev, utilized his philosophical profession of faith. In denouncing Russia's past and present he had quite unwittingly furnished weapons to the party which already intended to make a clean sweep of all that past. But, whereas Tchaadaev had discovered in Europe's Catholic past a stable foundation for future building, those who applauded his severe condemnation of Russia never dreamed of rebuilding the old European edifice : they planned complete destruction, the consummation of the revolution, the advent of a new mankind freed from any restraint, the discipline of the Church included. And if again ears were strained to catch rumours coming from France, it was to harken to Saint-Simon, and later to Fourier and Proudhon. In Moscow a small group of young people gathered to study the doctrines of Saint-Simon—it was directed by Herzen, who later headed the Russian revolutionary movement, and quite wrongly hailed Tchaadaev as a prophet, because the problem raised by him pertained to the philosophical and in no wise to the political order. The question was reduced to this : What part in history was Russia destined to

play ? Was she, indeed, entitled to any part outside
the great Roman communion ?

It was in reply to this question that Russia's
intellectual élite split into two groups, the conflicting
solutions of which divided Russian thought up to the
revolution. When the young intellectuals enlisted,
first under the colours of Schelling and, later, of
Hegel, the application of their ideas to Russia's
history landed them in two hostile camps, known
respectively as *Westernizers* and *Slavophils*.

The first continued the eighteenth century tradition : Russia, they believed, was a European country, the normal development of which had been
retarded by fortuitous circumstances, such as the
Tartar invasion, which had turned her face towards
Asia. Under Peter the Great she found her way
again, and was now to follow the evolution of the
Western nations which would be all the easier to do
since she had no mediæval traditions and had burst
into the " age of enlightenment " at one jump.
Viewed from this angle, a national religion was considered to have been a great boon, and the salvation
of the country from the centuries of " obscurantism "
which had so impeded the progress of the Latin
world. This was a new and curious aspect of the
traditional anti-Catholic bias, and, though the
argument used was a different one, eventually it
closely approximated to the old ideal of a national

religion. Anti-Christianity did not enter into the programme of these Westernizers (their extreme left wing excepted) : the Christianity the Russian Church professed was in their opinion quite compatible with the progressive evolution of mankind. They approved of everything in the Russian Church which separated her from Catholicism, particularly of the vagueness of her doctrinal teaching, her abstention from any activity in social life, and the implicit Protestant sympathies of many of her representatives. Was not Protestantism an improvement upon Catholicism ? . . . These Westernizers greatly admired the Renaissance and the Reformation, which had done away with mediæval " obscurantism." Faithful to the traditions of the Encyclopædists, they pictured mankind advancing in a straight line leading from darkness to light, a movement of ceaseless progress. Russia, being now on that line, had only to follow it ; in the meanwhile, until the coming of still more enlightened times, the inoffensive Church could be tolerated as embodying a venerable tradition, and also as being useful to look after the morals of the common herd. Hegel's philosophy was expedient in order to show that every existing phenomenon had its *raison d'être* as a starting-point for a future development.

This is a general outline of the ideology of these Westernizers. There were necessarily many different shades within a party that included simultaneously the most " advanced " revolutionary tendencies and a moderate liberalism which hoped for nothing beyond a slow evolution towards a European constitutional government : the attitude towards the State Church varied in accordance with the political programme of the particular group. But on one point all these groups in the Western party were in agreement—a denial to the Church of any predominating part ; a Christian mentality was unnecessary, as the secularization of the State had been a benefit and was to be pursued in the name of that free thought which was inseparable from all other civil liberties. This was, in fact, an echo of ideas which in Europe were being opposed to the Catholic revival.

The *Slavophils* rejected this ideology entirely. This party owed its origin to a nationalist reaction against the influence of French thought, the danger of which was seen first in Jacobinism and later in Catholic propaganda. This nationalism also found its philosophical definition of Russia's greatness in German idealism, in Schelling's " Universal Spirit," and Hegel's historical animism. The idea, transformed into an historical thesis, whereby Russia had a special soul in virtue of which she had a place apart from the rest of the world, was a Hegelian contribution to Slavophil ideas ; to it was joined the dream of the

Third Rome, resurrected with all its implications and clothed again in the mantle of Orthodoxy. Thus at one stroke Russia's entire past was not only justified, but glorified. The Byzantine heritage, so carefully preserved throughout the centuries, was the mystical leaven of the Russian consciousness. The epoch of Peter the Great was a deviation, a negation of the sacred mission. Now Holy Russia had found her road again and would proceed onward and upward ; not only would she reconquer the Byzantine heritage, but would join to it the entire world of the Slavs, her " brethren by blood and by faith." This pan-slavism gave the party its name of " Slavophil." It was a mixture of political imperialism, the religious conception of the Third Rome, and anti-Latinism. The religious element predominated : " Western Slavs " were considered brothers chiefly in the faith and the love shown them did not extend to the Poles—" renegades of Orthodoxy."

The Slavophils also presented many different shades. They had an extreme left wing akin to the revolutionary movement : it rejected the work of Peter and the whole autocratic *régime* said to have been inherited from the Tartars, and later consolidated by Western influence and the copying of Louis XIV and Frederick II ; it loathed Prussianized militarism, and longed for a great democratic federation of all Slavonic countries. Contrariwise, the extreme right saw in autocracy the priceless guarantee of Russian might, a wall protecting her against the subversive ideas of the " degenerate West " ; the monarch, ruling by the grace of God, was indeed the heir of Constantine and Justinian, the champion of Orthodoxy : he it was who continued to " gather the Russian land," adding to it the entire Slav world and beyond it the whole Christian East. But the distinctive trait of the Orthodox Tsar, as compared with his Byzantine predecessors, was that his power rested directly upon the Russian people, of whose sacred hopes he was the symbol. Preserved in the past from feudalism, Russia was also to be safeguarded from parliamentarism ; no intermediary was needed between the sovereign, God's anointed, symbol of the national unity, and the people—bearer of a great and mysterious mission, who had resisted the snares of Western civilization and treasured the precious pearl of Christian humility, promise of the final victory against Satan and his world, of the triumph of Orthodoxy.

Under this somewhat fantastic view of Russian history and the exaggerated idealization of the people there existed a grain of truth : the Slavophils were right to see in the rural population the predominating element of the nation : the compact mass of the peasantry (in the early nineteenth century

80 to 90 per cent. of the whole people) had certainly always determined the national psychology far more than did the town dwellers, who began to rise to some importance only in the eighteenth century. And they were also right when they accused their Westernizing antagonists of borrowing from Europe political notions which nothing in Russia's past justified, and especially of ignoring the religious foundation of the Russian mind. But they, too, were guilty of falsifying history by their undue idealization of the peasant and the rudimentary forms of his social life (such as common ownership), and by their conception of the people's religion : its incoherence and errors, often in flat contradiction with the doctrine of the Orthodox Church, totally escaped their notice.

So the Slavophil party represented a medley of confused ideas all converged towards the one centre of a national religion identified with the very essence of the Russian soul. This was the definite aspect which the hostility towards the Western world was to assume, a hostility towards Rome from the religious viewpoint, towards Europe as a whole from the political and social. This mystical particularism, tinged with messianism, admirably fitted in with an imperialism dreaming of a European hegemony and of the conquest of the East.

Beside this Slavophilism vacillating between different political parties there existed an official doctrine inspired by the Slavophils, formulated in 1832 by a well-known statesman, Count Uvarov, in three words : " Orthodoxy, autocracy, nation " (*pravoslavie, samoderzhavie, narodnost*). This was henceforth to be the official motto of the empire until its collapse in 1917. The word *narodnost* has a wider meaning than " nation " ; it implies not so much a racial as a spiritual affinity, a historical and ideological communion. Thus in the realm of home politics this motto did not presuppose the rejection of alien elements, but their assimilation into the Russian religion, language, and culture. Panslavism was to form the basis of a foreign policy the object of which was the " absorption of Slavonic streams in the Russian sea," to quote a verse of Pushkin. Lastly, in religion this battle-cry implied the old union of Church and State—though entirely in favour of the State, which became absolute master over the Church, identifying her with itself.

At first sight this official doctrine seemed to reject Peter's tradition of a secular State, but actually secularization had been so thorough that nothing could destroy it. Regimental colours were ornamented with sacred images, the soldier was to fight for " Faith, Tsar, and Motherland," even when the enemy was Christian ; but the school curriculum was completely secular, science uncompromisingly positivist, and the bureaucracy governing the State Christian only in name.

Suddenly a voice was heard denouncing the insufficiency of religious emotion bereft of a Christian conception of everyday life. In 1847 Gogol, a great satirist who was also a profound mystic, whose study of human depravity made him long for a high ideal and for a moral beauty, published his *Leaves from my correspondence*, in which he called for a deeper understanding of Christianity, an effort to Christianize daily life and social obligations, exposing at the same time the hollowness of the flowery phraseology so dear to exponents of "national Orthodoxy." There was a general outcry : indignation against Gogol was nearly as great as it had been against Tchaadaev : he was accused of preaching, of hypocrisy, was suspected of having fallen under Catholic influence in Rome, where he had resided for many years ; he, too, was declared to be mad.

It is interesting to compare his case with that of Tchaadaev : the latter was officially declared insane by order of the Tsar, and as a punishment. All liberal historians denounced this peculiar sentence as an act of intolerable despotism, yet one after another these same historians accused Gogol of a mystical lunacy only because he had dared speak of a Christianization of social life, had said that a secular spirit was in opposition to the inborn mysticism of the Russian people, and that Russia's true path lay in a conscious regeneration of the spirit through a Christian inward life and an understanding of the actual teaching of the Church.

Byelinsky, leader of the extreme left wing of Westernizers, wrote Gogol an indignant letter in which, among other arbitrary assertions, he declared that the Russian people were not at all religious, that they were not only anti-clerical, but anti-Christian, and ripe for the positivism which would free their minds from old superstitions. This is an example of how the theorizers of the time had lost touch with reality : to say that the Russian masses were devoid of a religious spirit was to ignore the evidence. Byelinsky's error is explained by the fact that he was one of the founders of a new social class, alien to any national tradition. Up to that time Russia's intellectual élite had been composed of country squires, deeply rooted in the soil ; now the spread of higher education created a new class of intellectual proletariat, completely uprooted from the soil.

About the middle of the nineteenth century this class, despite its numerical inferiority, constituted already a powerful public opinion ; it had no knowledge of the people, for it knew only the townsfolk : in its eyes the peasant was an abstract being which it idealized as an oppressed victim without ever really understanding his psychology—it saw him as the

" natural man " invented by the eighteenth century. This group rallied to the " Western " party because it had shed all national traditions and hoped to forward the cause of an Utopian socialism through the transplanting of European anti-clericalism into Russia. Thus the fight against religion became only another aspect of the struggle against the Government, which was identified with religious traditions, and European revolutionaries supplied the necessary arguments. The Slavophils, who were much closer to traditional Russian mentality, strove to unite a political democratism with the religious spirit inseparable from Russian nationalism, but, whilst endeavouring to find a line of demarcation between their own politico-religious conceptions and the official Cæsaro-papism, they succumbed to an exaggerated democratization of Christianity, substituting for the authority of the Church the principle of a private judgment of religious dogma. Studying the people's religion, they unconsciously came under the influence of an anarchical pseudo-mysticism manifest in their conceptions when they tried to define them, and elicited principles savouring more of the Protestant Reformation than of Eastern Orthodoxy. Thus, despite their admiration for the pre-Petrine traditions, the Slavophils had a hand in the "Lutheranization " of the Russian Church.

The extreme right of this party never tired of

praising the ideological originality of Russian Orthodoxy so easily adaptable to the official doctrine. If the Church had lately identified herself with the State it was, they said, because her distinctive feature was humility, as opposed to the arrogance of the Roman Church. However strange this insistence upon humility may seem in a mentality so permeated by national pride, it actually formed the basis of their conception of a Church which, of her own free will, had surrendered to the temporal power her authority and right of jurisdiction, and this not only because the temporal power was essentially identical to herself, but also because any intervention in worldly affairs was incompatible with her humility. The God-bearing Russian people as a whole was the very incarnation of this humility, and the true Russian, being lowly of heart, despised the attractions of Western civilization and of all worldly goods. Such assertions were a strange distortion of the Eastern Church in general, and of the Church of Russia in particular, but unconsciously they reflected the ancient conception of a Christianity contemptuous of the world and entrenched in some remote spiritual sphere. Again, and under a new form, the typical dualistic tendencies of the Russians came to the surface. The nineteenth century being too far removed from any monastic ideal, there was no longer question of seeking refuge in monasteries, but it was considered that the world itself, because of Russia's special grace of election, would find salvation in a humble interior righteousness. And if Russia was great and glorious it was only because of this essential meekness of hers ; she was hallowed by a true understanding of Christian humility which absolved her from the need of any other and more active virtues.

This naïve idealizing may raise a smile, yet throughout the nineteenth century it constituted the leaven of Russian thought, and in a slightly modified form is still at the bottom of the Russian mind, which cannot be appreciated without a knowledge of this religious nationalism as defined during the conflict with the Westernizers. Tyutchev, one of Russia's great poets, expressed these thoughts in well-known lines :

"These poor hamlets, this arid country. . . .
Beloved and patient land of the Russian people !
Never will the proud foreigner understand that
    which is reflected in and which glows mysteriously
    beneath thy humble poverty.
Bowed under the weight of the cross, garbed as
    a slave,
Blessing thee, the King of Heaven tramps thy
    highways."

Thus even literature, born of Western influence, was pervaded by the national element and remembered the old legend wherein Christ himself trod the

Russian earth. The fusion of nation and religion was as complete as in the fourteenth century.

But was this the religion of Sergius of Radonezh? Such a question would have surprised not only Slavophils but also the State Church. Had she not safeguarded her doctrine in all its integrity?—so different from the " heresy-ridden Latins." No one perceived the changes latent under externally unchanging forms. For long the Church had been only a liturgical rite, she had forgotten her own teaching : she even seemed unconscious of the imprecision of the statements of that teaching, always referring back to the authority of the Greek fathers—whom no one ever read. So the Slavophils, in the person of Khomyakov, attempted to set out a general conception of the Church in the divine economy, and of the special mission which devolved upon the Russian Church.

CHAPTER VIII

LAY THEOLOGY

THE Western current of Russian philosophical
thought developing along positivist lines, ended in
militant materialism, whereas religiously minded
Slavophilism was concerned with a kind of theology
compounded of Russian traditions and of speculations borrowed from German idealistic philosophy.
This mixture is typical of Khomyakov's writings,
which are disconcerting in their incoherence,
amateurishness, contradictions and false generalizations, yet arresting because of the writer's obvious
sincerity even in his mistakes ; their importance for
the history of Russian religious development cannot
be overestimated. Khomyakov was the first lay
theologian to wield so great an influence upon the
Church of Russia and her teachings.

Khomyakov (1804–1860) and his friend Kireevsky
headed the Slavophil movement, but whereas the
latter went so far in his vindication of the past as to
say that Muscovy had realized the ideal of a Christian State, Khomyakov's inherent honesty compelled
him to admit that Russia's past had as little in

common with an ideal Christianity as her present. The moral strength of the Russian people was not to be found in social life or in the external activities of the Church, but it was with Russia's soul that this Church was in complete harmony, and she had sowed in it seeds of a mystical universality diametrically opposed to the Catholicism of Rome. According to this conception Russia was an earthly counterpart of the Kingdom-not-of-this-world, whereas Rome had fashioned a theocratic idea subservient to temporal concerns. Rome's separation from the East was due to her assimilation of Roman law, in opposition to the very spirit of Christianity : she knew justice and not charity. And herein, according to Khomyakov and his school, lay Rome's fundamental error : she had introduced a judicial spirit into the doctrine of the Incarnation and into all man's relations to God. With a lawyer's dry thoroughness the Catholic Church had analyzed these relations, balanced good and evil, substituted logic for faith and charity. Juridicism, rationalism, such were in Khomyakov's opinion the salient features of the Roman " heresy," of which Protestantism with its complete rejection of a sacred tradition was an inevitable result.

Orthodoxy, on the contrary, had safeguarded the purity of Christianity because it had avoided precise definitions and was in no need of a visible authority in order to know the truth which reveals itself to a grace-enlightened intuition. It is useless to attempt to discover in Khomyakov's writings any definition of his idea of the Church : when he speaks of the one Church constituted of all the national Churches, from which " Romanism " had seceded, he has in mind a vague abstraction eluding any definition. It was nearer the conception of the " soul of a Church " than of the Body of Christ, and a nebulous soul, a vision in which the historical reality of the Church had been dissolved.

In short, Revelation was an intuition accepted by a collective conscience, the validity of dogma being vouched for only by this acceptance and sacraments existing only in so far as this collective conscience acknowledged their value. What is stranger still is that Khomyakov sincerely imagined that this shadow-Christianity was indeed the teaching of the Eastern Church, whereas it was only a philosophical idealism grafted upon the anarchical " mysticism " of Russian sectarianism. If he knew the Catholic Church only from crude distortions, he was also ignorant of the theology of his own Church, which he fondly imagined himself to be loyally serving whilst attributing to her notions that were not only alien to her doctrine but incompatible with the very conception of the Church. Without intending it, Russian religious traditionalism led to a rejection of the entire dogmatic framework of Christianity : christological Docetism, ever latent in the Russian Church, now transformed her into a bodiless phantom. In the heat of his anti-Catholic fervour, Khomyakov went so far as to declare that the Church could not be materialized, that to invest a particular place or episcopal see with authority was a grave heresy, for the Church's dwelling was the collective human soul : in fact, she was not a material reality, but an idea. In applying this principle to Russian messianism, Khomyakov transcended the *Third Rome* conception, now associated with official militant imperialism, the " Russian soul " itself becoming a kind of abstraction, trustee of an illusory dream. . . .

Some years after Khomyakov's death Samarin, one of his followers, declared him to have been a *doctor of the Church*, but this opinion was not endorsed by the general public, for whom his theories were too indefinite and unintelligible. It lay with the Russian Church to pronounce upon this matter, but she was only beginning to be concerned with theology and first she had to clear the ground. The ecclesiastical colleges wanted definitions of her fundamental teaching, so she had no time to trouble over varieties of opinion. The first serious work of the kind was Metropolitan Macarius's *Orthodox Dogmatic Theology* (1853), inspired by text-books in use in Western seminaries and an adaptation of scholasticism to the teaching of the Græco-Russian Church, a fact which caused the book to be suspected of " Latinism " ; moreover, its dry formulas were distasteful to the Russian mind, now attached to obscure generalizations. The *Orthodox Theology* of Philaret, Archbishop of Chernigov (1866), a controversial work directed against German exegesis, brought attention back to the history of dogmatic definitions, a matter also emphasized in the *Regulations for Ecclesiastical Academies* (1869). Philosophical speculations had no place in the ecclesiastical curriculum, whose programmes were solely for the instruction of the clergy and never crossed the threshold of their colleges. The Church was indifferent to " lay theology " ; and there was no authority to condemn distortions of Christian doctrines by thinkers whose audacity by far exceeded their competence.

Besides, the new era which was opening was unpropitious for theological discussion. Khomyakov was the representative of a generation of theorizers which vanished in the ideological turmoil of the reign of Alexander II, that turning-point of Russian history. It was a time of reform, the country was being remodelled on more liberal lines ; but extremists remained dissatisfied, and banded together to oppose the Government. This struggle lasted for half a century and ended only at the great revolution of 1917. The extremists, uncompromisingly materialist, were soon to find in Marxism their profession of faith. The more moderate groups refused to accept such subversive doctrines, and the bulk of the Westernizers' party evolved in the direction of a liberal nationalism, accepting a national religion along with other traditions. On this ground they met the Slavophils, whose pan-slavist ideals had been rudely shattered when the Russo-Turkish war of 1877–1878 revealed the fact that the " Slav streams " had not the slightest wish to be " absorbed in the Russian sea." The outcome of this disillusion was the consolidation of a narrower ideological nationalism, " messianism " undergoing a process of internal concentration all the more intensive now that Russia asserted herself in the world otherwise than by armed force.

In literature and other arts Russia could be justly proud of her universally acknowledged achievements ; she had demonstrated a specifically Russian culture, embracing philosophical speculation as well as the beautiful chant of her liturgy. Russia's attitude towards the Europe she had both loathed and admired underwent a great change now that new problems confronted her. Her eastward drive brought her to the foot of the Himalayas and to the coast of the Pacific : the conquest of the Amur region closely followed upon the fall of the last strongholds of the Caucasus and the subjection of Central Asia. So in the second half of the nineteenth century Russia found herself a formidable Asiatic Power, not a colonial empire in the European sense, but one homogenous block, the Asiatic portion of which disproportionately outbalanced the ancient Russian territories : to the ideological heritage of Justinian was added the realistic inheritance of Genghiz-Khan. A ferment of new ideas ensued which much later found expression in the *Eurasian* formulæ, though they were already apprehended by Soloviev when he questioned with misgiving whether Russia would be " the East of Xerxes or of Christ ? "

Above everything else Russia felt herself to be a world apart, and anti-Latinism now found new arguments. The immediate result of internal reforms was a strong democratization whereby the people's mentality influenced the intellectuals, and quite unexpectedly the radical party discovered allies among the unlettered adepts of rationalist sects which supported them in their struggle against the State and its Church.

In revolutionary circles religious problems connected with social questions were freely discussed, whilst at the other pole of Russian thought loyalty to the Church assumed the shape of a mystical, somewhat hazy religiosity which easily adapted itself to Khomyakov's musings ; while the Church herself was conscious of the deep divergence between her official time-serving and the monastic ideal.

We have spoken of the spiritual regeneration of the monasteries in the eighteenth century. A few decades later intellectuals found their way to these shrines of national religion. Khomyakov, and later Dostoyevsky and Soloviev, sat at the feet of the great *startzy* Macarius and the Ambrose of Optina monastery. Religion, quickened by the Slavophil leaven, got from the old ascetic teachings a new conception of the Church ; it perceived that by the words and example of her monks she, too, condemned the secular spirit which had contaminated the "white clergy," *i.e.*, the parish priests. The age-long contempt for this clergy had been an invincible obstacle in the way of the intellectuals' reconciliation with the Church ; now the ancient belief that the real Church was only in the monasteries was resurrected, and, as in the Middle Ages, people went there to breathe again the atmosphere of holiness.

But this monastic ideal was too aloof from daily life to be able to Christianize it ; it had little effect on the secular mentality, which it would not even attempt to combat—thus did it interpret its condemnation of the world. To the new intellectual, as to his Muscovite forefather, the monastery was but a passing impression, a short spell of recollection which was supposed to suffice to hallow a life lived outside the Church. Unconsciously, the idea of a religion free from any obligations and sanctions was sought there, and so the religious rebirth of the later nineteenth century corresponded to Khomyakov's ideas and assimilated them. National religion assumed its final aspect of an indefinite mysticism, completely wrapped up in the ritual of worship and totally indifferent to the Church's dogmatic substance, which was viewed as some kind of an imprecisely defined idealist philosophy. Russia's religious mission was conceived as the ulterior development of this mysticism through an absorption of all idealistic currents, Eastern as well as Western, excluding, naturally enough, Roman " juridicism." Russian messianism was now looking forward to a time when the mystical ideal it embodied would be the universal form of Christianity, and so it turned with closer attention to links broken from the great Roman tree, Anglicans and Old Catholics, among whom something was awakening which bid fair to bring them within the orbit of the Russian religious idea.

All this remained indefinite up to the end of the nineteenth century ; the State Church, though influenced, was not dominated by these currents. Alexander III was still on the throne, and a last effort was being made to ensure the triumph of the idea of " autocracy, Orthodoxy, nation," though without any too flagrant a departure from the official doctrine of the Church. This famous formula had a warm champion in Pobyedonostzev, procurator of the Holy Synod and incontestable *de facto* head of the Russian Church. Sympathy was shown to Old Catholics, courtesies exchanged with the Church of England, and a free hand was allowed to certain laymen to launch into theological discussions with strong unionist tendencies. Meanwhile, teaching in the ecclesiastical colleges was being Lutheranized, translations from Harnack, Sohm, Zahn, and other German scholars served as text-books, and all Catholic works were rigorously excluded. The hierarchy, trained in these schools, was favourably disposed towards notions which appeared to broaden Orthodoxy's horizons, whilst its traditional outward forms were retained ; on the other hand, lay thought was drawing nearer to the Church, whose doctrine seemed elastic enough to embrace the day-dreams of dilettante theologians.

Thus the problem facing the Russian conscious-ness in the last decades of the nineteenth century was complex. Through two centuries so many divergent elements had gone to its making that the elaboration of a synthesis was not easy ; and yet the Russian mind felt the urgency of some clear definition, for the growing revolutionary movement cast a dark cloud over the future. Religious particularism and universal messianism, national pride and anarchist trends, mysticism and rationalism, Europe and Asia, and many more apparently irreconcilable ideas clashed in a way which is best reflected in the writings of Dostoyevsky.

Those who speak of Dostoyevsky without knowing the ideological conflicts of which he is the outcome imagine him to have been a great originator of ideas. Actually his genius resides in the power of absorbing the most contradictory notions, of evoking longings deeply hidden in the Russian soul ; more thoroughly than any of his predecessors he fathomed the mysticism of the people's religion, discerning in it the elements both of anarchy and of Manichæism. Haunted by the problem of evil, he was indulgent towards the wickedness in the material world ; his tenderness towards sinners was exaggerated into an amoral indifference. Dostoyevsky's Christianity is, indeed, the semi-Manichæism which is the hyphen connecting Russia's supreme conception of religion, the monastic ideal, with the sombre traditions of sectarian " mysticism." To this he added the messianism fostered by intellectual currents deriving from other social layers. He strove to express everything, and that is why his work is a welter of unsolved problems : in this he reflected the spirit of his time. He sought frantically for a synthesis of

Russian thought which would supply a definition for a universal Christianity hazily perceived as a theocracy wherein the State would be merged into the Church, which, in her turn, would be an abstraction devoid of any material reality. Dostoyevsky would have been unable to give a coherent account of his own ideas, for he was himself the incarnation of the irreconcilable conflict between Christianity and Manichæism, which is at the very root of Russian religion. He chose the form of the novel as a medium for the expression of his theological conceptions because the interplay of his characters allowed him to voice the agonizing contradictions of his own thoughts. His genius showed him the gulfs, but could never lift him as high as the Unity.

Soloviev attempted to give a substance to the theocratic dream. Alone among the great Russian thinkers, he had a thorough philosophical training and was able to distinguish between the abstract idea and its realization. Emerging from Slavophil mists, he followed in the steps of Tchaadaev, and understood that in the Roman ideal Catholic Christianity had already reached a concrete reality. But even Soloviev was unable to rid himself of a residuum of anarchistic " mysticism " ; his personal convictions led him back to the Universal Church, without hindering him from indulging in speculations transcending the limits of the authentic Christian tradition. Beyond the dogmas of the Church he sought to rediscover the ancient *gnosis*, with its emphasis on the primordial opposition of the masculine and feminine principles, wisdom, the emanation of the divine Unknown, and complement of the Creating Word. This side of Soloviev's philosophical and theological writings had a decisive influence over subsequent Russian thought, far greater indeed than his Catholic convictions, which were never taken seriously in Russia.

Next to these two greatest of Russian thinkers hovers the shadow of Tolstoy, considered in the West to have been a typical representative of Russian Christianity. This is a great mistake. Tolstoy reflected only one, and the least characteristic, aspect of the people's religion—that of rationalist sectarianism. Of all Russian writers, Tolstoy is the one who most lacks mystical feeling, is the most alien to the traditions of the national religion, the least capable of understanding them : Europe shared this lack of understanding, and that is why he is considered to be the spokesman of a religion of which he actually was only the faintest echo. The tremendous influence of Tolstoy in the Russia of his day is precisely due to his support of religious rationalism, vanguard of the revolutionary movement which allied itself with the sects to fight the State Church and to undermine the Cæsaro-papist empire.

Thirty years ago anyone could see that the structure of the Russian State was becoming unsafe. Philosophical thought assumed an apocalyptic trend ; Rozanov's mystical sensuality voiced the prevailing uneasiness, as did the passionate discussions about the social *rôle* of the Church carried on by those intellectuals who were the agnostics of yesterday. As a century earlier, mystical sectarianism affected the upper classes, and religious speculation held an important part in the great political and moral crisis which immediately preceded the explosion. Champions of national tradition discussed the regeneration of the Church, her emancipation from secular influence, and demanded the restoration of the Moscow patriarchate. The opposing camp caught hold of this idea, using it as a weapon to forward the separation of Church and State in order to weaken the latter by the loss of its sacred character. The question of a patriarchate became neutral ground whereon the most conflicting ideas met, and the Government reluctantly promised to call a council of the Russian Church, which would have inevitably led to the abolition of the generally detested synod and the restoration of the patriarchal see.

The official motto of " autocracy, Orthodoxy, nation " whirled like a dry leaf in the revolutionary hurricane. The abstract ideal of the " nation " was being undermined by the claims of national minorities, " autocracy " capitulated before the demand of constitutional reforms, and " Orthodoxy " was found to be the nervous centre where ideas more violent than lucid were in conflict. The " pre-conciliary " commission, appointed by the Government as early as 1905 to prepare for the council, met amidst a storm of complaints and aggressive demands. Politics intervened and the " white " (parochial) clergy bitterly confronted the " black " clergy, the monks and bishops, who had hitherto been the only actual representatives of the Church and beneficiaries of all her privileges. So when the collapse of the imperial power set free all centrifugal forces, the Church lost her unity and the hastily convened council was actually controlled by the secular element which had for so long oppressed her. The patriarch's election was only symbolic, for no reconstruction was possible at a time when alone disruptive forces were in operation. The Russian Church, which had shared all the vicissitudes of the State and also its greatness, followed it in its fall and drifted upon the revolutionary tide which was soon to become for her a torrent of blood.

CHAPTER IX

CONCLUSION

SUCH was the way of Russia's religious conscious-ness through the centuries until the revolution brutally destroyed all her slow and laborious evolution. This concluding chapter outlines the painful happenings which, during these last twenty years, have bewildered and upset Russia's religious mentality.

We have said that in the first years of this century all political parties agreed as to the urgency of a thorough overhauling of the entire administrative structure of the Church. Some visualized it as a still greater secularization of the State and the elimination of every vestige of its religious past, whilst for others it was the Church which had to be freed from the State's oppressive tutelage. There was unanimity upon the necessity of separating State from Church, but none as to the shape such a reform was to take. The majority desired the abolition of the synodal system and the restoration of the Moscow patriarchate; a considerable minority, however, feared that this restoration would strengthen the authority of the Church. Such opponents of the patriarchate were to be found not only among the indifferent or lukewarm laity, but also among the secular clergy. This so-called "white" clergy was jealous of their "black" brethren (monks), and dreaded an increase of power in the hands of the hierarchy, consisting exclusively of monks. They were supported by intellectuals who, though faithful to the Church, were nevertheless strongly influenced by Khomyakov and the other lay theologians who taught that the authority of the Church was in no wise vested in the hierarchy but in the *sobornost* (conciliarity, œcumenicity), constituted by the agglomerate body of the faithful. From this point of view a remoulding of the organization of the Church was desired so that a powerful lay element would participate in her administration. These laymen intended to infuse a "new spirit" into the Church, a fact which shows how strongly Protestantism had influenced the Slavophil religious mentality. Prince Troubetzkoy, a deep thinker and loyal Christian, had said a few years earlier that these proposed reforms "seemed more in keeping with the independent sects than with the Orthodox Church. This idea of democratization—election of priests by their flocks, an elected hierarchy, married bishops, and so forth, earnestly advocated by Slavophils—bears witness to a faulty understanding of the very spirit of the Church. . . . Also in the controversies of Slavophils with Western religious denominations is their Protestant bias only too obvious." [1]

This was a true definition of the mind governing the circles which clamoured for urgent and radical reforms. But when the Imperial Government consented to convene a pan-Russian council to heal the wounds of the Church, and whilst a " pre-conciliary commission " intended to pave the way for this convocation was constituted within the Synod, it became immediately evident that the atmosphere was too charged to allow of any peaceful work. So the commission was dissolved pending new orders, and the council indefinitely postponed. During the following decade the religious crisis reached a more acute stage, for these years coincided with the tragic affair of Rasputin, his incursion into all matters concerning the Church, whilst the hierarchy looked on powerless, or, in some cases, debased itself by a servile complicity.

According to the terse pronouncement of one archbishop, the Church resembled a sick man burning with fever. This is the reason why she played for safety when at the height of the war the internal crisis brought on the downfall of the imperial *régime :* her first thought was for herself

---

[1] Letter to C. Leontiev by which he severed his connections with the Slavophils.

and not for the *régime* of which she had formed an integral part. Subsequently it became expedient to exaggerate the " counter-revolutionary " attitude of the clergy ; actually, in the first days of the revolution, the secular clergy, with few exceptions, were definitely sympathetic to the great change, and even the higher hierarchy was not always unfavourable to it. At the first meeting of the Synod after the proclamation of a Provisional Government some of its members, archbishops, threw out the imperial chair, which symbolized the sovereign's invisible presence. They seemed at first to overlook the fact that the new procurator, nominee of the Provisional Government, treated them with scantier ceremony even than did the old procurator who had represented the " Lord's anointed."

Had this *régime*, constituted in February, 1917, been stabilized, it would easily have carried on the domination of the old State over the Church. But under the irrepressible onslaught of anarchy the entire social structure was crumbling, and it became urgent to preserve anything which could stem this tidal wave of destruction. A council of the Church was hastily convened, all the difficulties which had appeared insuperable twelve years earlier being brushed aside—canonical niceties were in no wise the concern of those who hoped that the Church would be able to fight the social revolution. Not only was the laity strongly represented, but it also played a predominant part in the council, especially since it numbered some of the outstanding political personalities of the day. In fact, the council was a kind of ecclesiastical counterpart of the Provisional Government, and intended to become a bulwark of liberal nationalism against Socialist internationalism. This political aspect of the council had a decisive influence upon the ultimate fate of the Russian Church. She allied herself officially, not with the old monarchical order which still had numerous zealous partisans, nor with the Socialism to which some of the secular clergy adhered, but with the men who, like their predecessors, the French Girondins, had engineered the revolution and were to be devoured by it.

This explains the spirit of the reforms and the character of the ecclesiastical structure elaborated by the council. Its fundamental idea was a kind of parliamentarism. Gradually all the participants sanctioned the restoration of the patriarchate, though the motives prompting their decision differed widely. Some hoped it would incorporate vestiges of a monarchical principle, others—more numerous— saw in it primarily and predominantly a break with the past, a challenge not to Cæsaro-papism only, but to any attempt to restore a monarchy *de jure divino*. The power of the patriarch was carefully restricted, so as to destroy the monarchical principle within the Church itself. This was one of the strangest paradoxes of those strange times : after lengthy and fully justified recriminations against the synodal system it was precisely this system which was chosen for the re-organization of the Church elaborated by this council in 1917. The patriarch was set up as the head of the Russian Church, but entirely dependent upon a representative system obviously inspired by the idea of two chambers. The " upper chamber " was to be a permanent Synod of twelve bishops, presided over by the patriarch. It was to deal with questions of faith and ritual. The whole administration and executive power was vested in a " supreme ecclesiastical assembly " of fifteen members, three of whom were bishops chosen among the members of the Synod, one monk representing the monasteries, five representatives of the secular clergy, though not necessarily priests (clerics in minor orders were qualified for election), and six laymen. Moreover, a council in which the actual authority of the Church was vested was to meet every three years. In the intervals between such councils all important matters were to be settled at plenary meetings of the Synod and the supreme assembly.

Thus it was a kind of parliamentary system, devoid of any power of maintaining a proper balance, for

the right of *veto* conceded to the patriarch was
merely nominal. The one place allotted to the
monks was a mockery when we remember the great
part the monasteries had played in Russian history.
It was clear that all actual power would be in the
hands of the laity, supported by the representatives
of the parish clergy. In short, this was not the
needed reform, but a decisive step towards a Protestant Reformation.

Such an ecclesiastical system was utterly incapable
of putting up any strong resistance to the forces of
disruption ; moreover, in the revolutionary turmoil
the most radical reforms failed to satisfy anyone.
The position taken up by the Church provoked
bitter criticism in the conservative camp, and was
the cause of an anti-clericalism which temporarily
alienated from her such elements as would otherwise
have been her staunchest supporters. The greater
menace, however, came from the opposite camp,
where the reforms were considered insufficiently
drastic. That the influence of the monasteries had
been undermined was not enough—a demand was
advanced that bishops should no longer be chosen
from among the monks alone, and that married
priests be also qualified for episcopal consecration.
Parish priests claimed the right to modify the
liturgy at their own fancy, and the authority of the
hierarchy was ignored : the Church was in the

throes of a kind of madness, but this cyclone which threatened to sweep everything away eventually led to salutary results. Ecclesiastical authority, attacked from every side, finally weathered the storm.

Lacking actual power, Patriarch Tikhon enjoyed a moral authority which allowed him to dominate the turmoil when the trend of events freed him from elected organizations which so impeded his work : civil war and a state of general chaos prevented the periodical convocation decreed by the statute of 1917. Members of the Synod and the supreme assembly could not be re-elected at the fixed times, and upon the expiration of their term of office the patriarch remained the sole lawful holder of authority, provisionally at least. On the other hand, the moderate Republican party with which the council had allied itself in 1917 had disappeared, and the Church was now alone, facing a power whose hatred of Christianity was implacable. The first symptoms of persecution were being experienced, some martyrs had shed their blood, and a wave of brutal anti-religious manifestations had swept over the land. The faithful gathered closely around the shepherd in whom they saw the incarnation of the national and religious ideal which the country had believed in throughout so many centuries, whilst the very zeal of the reformers soon carried them outside the Church. The Soviet Government encouraged the organization of such groups as the " Living Church," the " Renovated Church," and others. These not only became a grave menace to the Patriarchal Church, but encroached upon her rights and dispossessed her of a great part of the Church buildings, seized by the Living Church under the Government's auspices. Yet all this was beneficent to the moral prestige of the patriarch, for these groups absorbed the most refractory " modernist " elements. Henceforth the innovation of married bishops, the scandal of priests celebrating freaky services and so on ceased to be upon her : the indignation and contempt of the faithful were poured upon the " modernist " sects, whilst the patriarch's authority, living symbol of ancient traditions, greatly increased. So, when plunder of the Church (under the pretext of aid for the victims of the famine of 1921–1922) and hideous desecrations were followed by bloody persecution, the faithful looked to their pastors to defend them or share their fate. If in old times the monks alone commanded the real respect of the people, now their devotion went to the humblest parish priest when he was prepared to accept the martyr's crown. But something greater than reverence was felt for the patriarch and the higher hierarchy.

So circumstances contributed to strengthen the central authority now exclusively wielded by Patriarch Tikhon. At the time of his arrest in 1922 he chose a provisional successor, transferring to him " the government of the Church pending the convocation of a council." There was no mention of a permanent synod, and still less of any supreme assembly : virtually the constitution of 1917 had been abrogated. Three years later, on the eve of his death (1925), the patriarch seemed to confirm the situation by appointing three bishops to shoulder his responsibilities until the time when the convocation of a council, necessary for a new election, was possible.

Shortly afterwards Metropolitan Peter, who, as *locum tenens*, had succeeded Tikhon, was also arrested. His temporary successor, Metropolitan Sergius, still heads the Church in the U.S.S.R. as " acting *locum tenens* of the patriarchal see." Anxious to consolidate his own position and propitiate some of the refractory bishops, he reverted to a partial restoration of the synodal system by the creation of a " patriarchal synod " where bishops sit by turn at bi-annual sessions. Since 1927 this organization has undergone modifications, though its fundamental principle—a compromise between the patriarchal authority of pre-Petrine days and the constitutional exactions of 1917—has been maintained. Only a council can finally solve the question of the organization of the Church, and its convocation has become problematic, not only because of the political situation, but as much because of canonical differences due to deep dissensions within the very bosom of the Russian Church. The revolution and ensuing civil war drove part of the episcopate out of the country, and they and their flock became virtually cut off from any regular intercourse with the see of Moscow. The exiled bishops constituted themselves a kind of permanent synod, sitting at Karlovtzy in Yugo-slavia, and presided over by the Metropolitan Anthony. Increasing political differences strongly influenced the relations of this emigré synod and the patriarch and his representatives.

At first the position of these bishops was only the natural and inevitable reaction against the concessions to the spirit of the times which had marked the early days of the revolution and been so calamitous for the dignity and authority of the Church. Then the outbreak of civil war deepened the gulf between those who sought to establish a *modus vivendi* for the Church by submitting to the demands of the Soviet *régime* and the others who would have nothing to do with a persecuting and openly godless Government. Most of the emigré bishops threw in their lots with the monarchists ; in this they only followed the ideological evolution of the emigré masses : for as the tragedy of Russia gradually revealed itself under a tyranny which mercilessly destroyed all her past, drowning the national ideal in blood, this ideal shone forth with a renewed glory. The mistakes of the past were forgiven and forgotten, and only bitter regret was felt for the loss of what had been insufficiently treasured and safeguarded. It is this very natural psychology of the emigrés which inspired the professions of monarchist faith of the exiled bishops, and which the Soviets welcomed as a pretext for accusing the whole clergy of counter-revolution. On the other hand, Metropolitan Sergius emphasized his conciliatory attitude towards the powers-that-be by a public denial of the existence of any religious persecution in the U.S.S.R. This declaration caused a complete rupture between the See of Moscow and the bishops in exile, whilst in Russia herself a considerable clerical group refused to obey the metropolitan's injunctions demanding a loyal attitude towards the persecuting Government.

The difference between the Church in Russia and her offshoots abroad was only deepened by political and canonical disagreements. The monarchist declarations of the Karlovtzy Synod antagonized the clergy and laity faithful to the principles of 1917. And exile unavoidably brought out the national question, the historical stumbling-block of Eastern Christianity. Orthodox dioceses in the new States formed from provinces of the old Russian Empire demanded autonomy on the strength of the principle that the limits of a Church corresponded to the political boundaries of the State. Thus were born the autocephalous Churches of Poland and Finland, and the autonomies of Latvia and Estonia, so many branches broken off the old trunk of the Russian Church. But worse was to come when the bishops of considerable Russian refugee groups in the U.S.A., China and Western Europe also demanded autonomy, on the ground that there existed no canonical precedent to justify the jurisdiction claimed by the Karlovtzy Synod. Metropolitan Eulogius, of Paris, placed himself under the jurisdiction of the Patriarch of Constantinople, an unprecedented thing in the annals of the Russian Church since the establishment of the Moscow patriarchate in the sixteenth century. Dissensions within the emigré Church grew and resulted finally in a cessation of intercommunion. After long and painful quarrels, the formation of separate jurisdictions, and so forth, partial reconciliation in 1935 re-established intercommunion, though the existing division was confirmed. For the time being the Russian Church in exile is split into four independent jurisdictions: the Balkans, America, the Far East, and Western Europe (with its see in Paris). The last is nominally subjected to the Patriarch of Constantinople. If to these four groups are added the autocephalous Churches of Poland, Finland, etc., it is easy to appreciate the extent of the dismemberment of the old Church of Russia and the difficulties a future council will encounter when the canonical position of this dismembered Church has to be dealt with.

The foregoing helps to explain the shocks which the Russian religious consciousness has experienced in the last eighteen years. The sight of the Church at first given to politics, then torn by bitter controversy in exile, was not one to calm the unrest caused by the overwhelming national catastrophe. The incursion of the laity into questions pertaining to the Church made matters worse, for then political passions dominated not only problems of jurisdiction, but also purely ideological questions. Whilst the greater part of the emigré Church strives to safeguard traditions which will enable them to restore their connection with the past, another group tends to develop the "modernist" spirit of the Khomyakov school and seeks a *rapprochement* with Protestantism, especially with the Church of England. This group has one thing in common with the traditionalists—the renovation of the Russian Church when the course of political events permits the reunion of the Churches in exile with whatever remains of the Mother Church in Russia : and the whole future of the Russian Church depends upon the way this reunion is carried out. The religious situation in Russia proper when persecution ceases promises to be very complex and fraught with unexpected developments.

In the U.S.S.R. the first onslaught of the godless took the faithful unawares when quarrels were rending the Church and causing numerous apostacies : many left her to swell the ranks of sectarianism, Baptists especially [1] were reaping a rich harvest. For half a century the State Church had painfully struggled against them, and now, every barrier broken down, it looked as if the Baptist torrent would carry off the bulk of the people. The menace was the greater because of the Soviet Government's eagerness to support any opposition against the Church. Therefore in the earlier persecutions Baptists were unmolested, and even enjoyed a certain freedom of propaganda. Curiously enough, their progress was impeded by their immunity from persecution, for when it became more ruthless the people flocked back to the Orthodox Church, which was gaining a new and tremendous prestige in their eyes. Moreover, the Government was not slow to discard the mask of religious indifference : Marxism manifested its implacable hatred of all Christianity ; tolerance was thrown aside, and sectarians put on an equal footing with all other believers.

[1] As has been said (Chapter VI) Baptists, known as *Stunda*, came to Russia in the middle of the nineteenth century. They are strongly supported by their American and English co-religionists, who founded a special Russian Missionary Society, particularly active in the Border States and among needy emigrés. (Transl.)

For a few years the godless triumphed : the timid and lukewarm were carried away by the flood of irreligion, and brigades of " militant godless " jubilantly drew up lists of persons who had " repudiated all religion." This break with Christianity was due not only to ruthless persecution, but also to the bewilderment of simple folk who, witnessing the desecration of all they held holy and the impunity of the sacrilegious, began to doubt of God. . . .

But if apostacies were numerous they were beneficent in cleansing the Church of all but the healthiest elements, which rallied to her as to the only stronghold of Christian faith, guardian of public and private morality, and of all the dear traditions now so cruelly trampled upon. As in the early days of the revolution, when the intellectual classes had been drawn towards the Church, so now the same happened among the people at large, even in places where the influence of rationalist sects had been strongest.

The years which followed until the Five-Year Plan had been launched was a time when the Church enjoyed a prestige she had never known since the days of *raskol*. In the countryside, especially, the peasants, disappointed of the benefits promised by the revolution, were in an opposition to the Soviet *régime* which took the shape of a stubborn loyalty to their persecuted Church. This furnished a pretext for a new and more violent offensive of the godless in connection with the collectivization of agriculture. In smashing the resistance of the peasants the Government started with the rural clergy, whom it accused of inciting the peasants to revolt, and denounced all Christians as being of an anti-Communist spirit. It was also considered that the collectivized peasants, dispossessed of their lands, were thereby incorporated in integral Socialism, incompatible with religion. *Kolkhozy* could have nothing to do with churches and clergy : this was why sacred buildings were either destroyed or put to other uses. The clergy were deported or massacred under the flimsy pretext of " counter-revolutionary plots." The first Five-Year Plan was to " do away with all traces of religion." The tribulations of this ruthless persecution were increased by the uncertainty as to the real attitude of the head of the Church, who had signed an agreement with the Soviets. Some members of the hierarchy and clergy who repudiated this agreement were deported, and again there was a mass exodus of distracted laity from the Church. Some gave up and were enlisted in the godless, but the majority, fired by mystical exaltation, stood firm. So when this policy drove numbers more out of the Church they were a gain neither for atheism nor for the rationalist sects, but for the numerous branches of " mystical " sectarianism.

When everything they had held most sacred was destroyed the Russian peasants in the twentieth century reverted to their ancestral mentality. Rumours of apocalyptic visions spread, prophets and prophetesses sprang up, people journeyed to out-of-the-way places in quest of mysterious *startzy*, guardians of the truth. In former days this fervour would have found a natural home in the monasteries, but these were no more : *nothing has survived of the many thousands of monasteries which covered the old Russia.* Their buildings have either been razed to the ground or turned into anti-religious museums. Monks and nuns were evicted and deported, many died in concentration camps ; and the people, deprived of their spiritual leaders, turned again to the latent sources of popular religion—the visionaries, *vurodivye*, who revived all the characteristics of anarchical " mysticism." Even in the towns, notwithstanding the ceaseless observation of a well-organized system of espionage, the presence of mystical sects was apprehended everywhere and one heard again rumours of *khlysty* " ships." In prisons and concentration camps, where the victims of persecution were numbered by tens of thousands, it was not generally Christians resigned to martyrdom that one met with, but fanatical sectarians full of contempt and hatred for their persecutors—" servants of anti-Christ "— and prepared to defy them.

At the end of the first Five-Year Plan the Government had to admit that, so far from " liquidating " the remnants of religion, they were further from their object than a decade earlier. " The end of religion " was again on the programme of the second quinquennial plan, but these were empty words. Actually since 1933 the Government has had to make concessions to religion : the brutal destruction of all village churches was given up ; in order to appease the peasants in revolt against collectivization this was separated from anti-religious activity and the survival of many village churches was conveniently overlooked. Violent methods were discarded ; raids on houses by young Communists in search of ikons, noisy meetings near the churches to disturb the services, even the blasphemous processions formerly organized and encouraged by the Government, were prohibited. These measures manifest an anxiety to remove temporarily a cause of deep irritation, but they are also due to another reason : the leaders of the godless confessed that where a church was destroyed mystical sectarianism sprung up, and its swift dissemination was such that it presented a greater danger for the *régime*. This sectarianism, concealed under the most divergent aspects, penetrated to the very citadels of atheism, so the Government considered it expedient to relax its pressure upon the Church, which was easier to watch and was, moreover, ready to temporize. As in the early years of the revolution the Government had backed the rationalist sects against the Church, now there has been a tendency for two or three years to legalize the Established Church to a certain extent in order to push back the advance of the " mystical " sects.

Such is the real cause of a superficial semi-tolerance which is mistaken abroad for a sign of an evolution of the Soviets' religious policy. Actually no essential modification can take place whilst the official ideology is grounded upon Marxism, which is absolutely incompatible with any religion, a fact the party leaders have repeatedly stressed in their formal declarations. The Church is only tolerated as provisionally useful, as a lesser evil. The position made for her precludes any possibility of her ever becoming dangerous, the avowed object being to let her " die a natural death," according to the words of a leader of the godless. This " natural death " consists in making impossible a normal supply of clergy by destruction of all seminaries, the prohibition of religious teaching, the denial to all clerics (even in minor orders) and their families of all rights (including the right to work), the strict application of the fiscal system to religious buildings, which renders their upkeep prohibitive ; lastly, the accusation of " secret counter-revolutionary activities " always hanging like a sword of Damocles over the heads of the faithful and their pastors, and the seizing of any pretext for mass arrests and deportations. Under this terror the Church is no longer a potential danger, and the Government has no reason for alarm if a few faithful meet in the few churches left them. And, anyhow, church-going is made difficult by the compulsory labour of both sexes and the abolition of Sundays : the Communist "rest-days" never coincide with the Christian holy days. But at some evening services, especially the Easter midnight Mass, churches are crowded. Tourists who observe these crowds have mistakenly believed them a sign of a new policy of tolerance. This filling of churches twice or thrice a year is due also to the decreased hostility of a great number of the faithful towards the Metropolitan Sergius. Whilst there were still refractory parishes, people worshipped there irrespective even of distance, but in 1933, the last churches of the other jurisdictions having been closed, the people preferred to return, however unwillingly, to the patriarchal obedience sooner than be deprived altogether of religious services, especially of the Easter solemnity. The Government's pretended tolerance is intended to mislead foreign public opinion : it is but a mask behind which the persecution has never ceased. The steady decrease in religious marriages, the moral anarchy, the giving up of all habits of a Christian life, are an indication of the colossal weakening of the Church's influence.

We repeat, the stronghold of religious fervour in the U.S.S.R. is not within the Orthodox Church, but in the " mystical " sects. The deepest manifestation of the people's religion is expressed in them, and they are waging a fight to the death against the materialism of Soviet actuality—and final victory will be with them. The Government is terrified to see their influence penetrating into the schools, even those most deeply permeated by militant atheism. The young generation, though inoculated with this atheism as an irrefutable doctrine, is accessible to the propaganda of religious " mysticism." For two years the anti-religious press has been pointing out this menace with an ever-growing concern, and in the many prisons where clergy and faithful of all religious confessions are herded together, one meets many groups of young people accused of participating in secret associations inspired by some obscure religious ideal.

Thus persecution has given birth to a religious movement which is not only a threat to Communism, but to the Russian Church also. When the day comes for her painfully to reconstruct her lost unity she will be confronted by a dense growth of " free sects," and this problem will be more acute than it ever was before.

In former times sectarianism had been kept in

check by the State's identification with the Church and by the prestige of the secular traditions of that Church. In a regenerated Russia this prestige will have suffered gravely, and the Church now carries the germs of further discord generated by the "modernist" tendencies spoken of above. She will experience great difficulty in reviving and consolidating her authority and influence in face of the centrifugal forces whose action is to-day so apparent.

Heated discussions upon doctrinal questions have been carried on around the Paris Theological Institute, and it is clear that the hierarchical authority is being undermined in the emigré Church. A yet stormier time is in store for the Church of Russia when the time for her reconstruction arrives. The "modernists" are not concerned with problems of external organization, but with the fundamental question of the *magisterium* of the Church, with the criterion of truth necessary for the integrity of dogmatic teaching.

No prophecy is possible. We can only express the ardent prayer and hope that the blood of innumerable martyrs, the heroism of so many confessors, will preserve the threatened unity and direct the Church of Russia along the paths of her real traditions. May these resurrected traditions lead her towards the only unity against which the gates of Hell will never prevail.